The

CONNECTED

Generation

**How Christian Leaders Around the World Can
Strengthen Faith & Well-Being Among 18–35-Year-Olds**

Funding for this research was made possible by the generous support of World Vision. Barna Group was solely responsible for data collection, analysis and writing of the report. The views expressed in this publication do not represent those of World Vision.

TABLE OF CONTENTS

Preface

My life has provided plenty of opportunities to push past assumptions and differences. When I moved back to the U.S. at the age of 18, I spoke only Spanish after having spent most of my childhood in Latin America. In my career, I've known the feeling of being the only executive at the conference table with an accent. I've sensed the weight of bias—and my own has gotten in the way, too. Raising two daughters with special needs, I'm always discovering new limitations I have unconsciously placed on them.

But I wholeheartedly believe that we are all one in Christ (Galatians 3:28), and that our faith should compel us to reach beyond stereotypes and work toward mutual understanding.

Millennials are one group that is often misunderstood and all too easy to judge—especially with regard to their faith. Although cynicism toward this generation abounds, I do not share it. I believe Jesus is lighting fires in the hearts of young people, just as he has done with all generations since he walked on this earth. World Vision wants to engage them in striving to realize God's plan for the world, particularly in fragile places where even a small act can make a huge impact.

That's why we commissioned this study from Barna Group. Understanding 18–35-year-olds and separating fact from assumption enables World Vision, and the Church at large, to help unleash young people's passion for Jesus. We want to equip faith leaders to connect and collaborate with this generation. The good news is that these young adults have great potential to change the world. They are globally minded and quick to embrace causes they believe in. Driven by a sense of humanitarian responsibility, they are personally invested in what's happening beyond their communities.

However, many are dissatisfied with their church experiences, longing for congregations to do more to fight injustice and make a significant impact on poverty.

When we understand these perspectives, we can reach

EDGAR SANDOVAL SR.
President and Chief Executive Officer,
World Vision U.S.

across the gap. I see a tremendous opportunity to authentically connect with this generation and their passion to live Jesus' calling in Matthew 25, to care for the hungry and thirsty, the stranger and those in need of clothing, the sick and imprisoned.

Engaging this generation within the body of Christ is an urgent assignment. The Church is the greatest God-ordained force for holistic transformation, able to penetrate cultural barriers and bring the hope of Jesus to all nations. And the Church's strength is its diversity, uniting people of all backgrounds and ages in bearing witness to Christ. Intergenerational and intercultural understanding strengthens churches for this mission. We need each other. Instead of dismissing Millennials for their perceived differences, let's believe in them and learn from them as together we realize our purpose in the kingdom of God.

Introduction

For more than a decade and across multiple projects, Barna has kept a close eye on the generation known as Millennials (defined in the United States as those born between 1984 and 1998). We've watched them navigate new technology, develop passions for community and justice, and balance particularly high ideals and ambitions. Our recent research has tracked their entrance into adulthood, career and family—and, among a significant proportion, a simultaneous departure from religion. We see similar trends now among the leading edge of Gen Z (born between 1999 and 2015), who so far are even less inclined toward religion than their Millennial peers. Pastors have told us their churches feel an urgency to reach these generations, yet struggle to gain their attention and commitment, particularly in a secularizing U.S., where Barna's research has been concentrated.

Faith leaders aren't the only ones seeking a greater understanding of these young adults. The stereotypes—some more fair than others—have stacked up, making Millennials, and Gen Z beyond them, a source of resentment at worst or bemusement at best. But the re-ality is that members of this age cohort are hardly "the next generation" anymore. Newcomers no longer, they are a formidable and present force, actively shaping the future of our industries, politics, arts, neighborhoods and, yes, churches. What values do they bring with them, and what kind of world are they already building?

Barna partnered with World Vision, a leading voice in global activism with a shared vision of engaging the next generation, to dramatically widen—and focus—the lens with which we view young adults around the world. We interviewed more than 15,000 adults ages 18 to 35 in 25 countries and nine languages, asking them about their goals, fears, relationships, routines and beliefs. This report represents an initial, comprehensive summary of those findings, a primer of sorts about a group we're calling *The Connected Generation*.

These respondents all have at least one thing in common in addition to their age: an internet connection. Though some themes vary by country and context, there are other similarities across borders. In the following articles, you'll meet maturing respondents who don't just want to be "reached"— they want to be involved and make a difference. Many of these driven adults are wary and weary, wrestling with questions, longing for deeper relationships and facing significant societal, professional and personal obstacles. Yet we see that faith is one important factor associated with their well-being, connection and resilience. When—or, for many, if—they walk into a church, they'll need concrete teaching from leaders they can trust and meaningful opportunities to contribute to a faith community.

Through these pages, Barna's aim is not only to help the global Church to better understand 18–35-year-olds around the world, but to truly partner with them in discipleship and encourage their leadership. We invite you to join us in learning more about, and from, this connected generation.

Methodology

This study is based on online, representative public opinion surveys conducted by Barna Group. A total of 15,369 respondents ages 18 to 35 across 25 countries were surveyed between December 4, 2018, and February 15, 2019. Sample distribution based on continent and country are shown below.

North America
- United States (2,000)
- Canada (1,000)

Africa
- South Africa (750)
- Nigeria (512)
- Kenya (300)
- Ghana (462)

Asia
- South Korea (500)
- India (500)
- Philippines (250)
- Indonesia (500)
- Singapore (500)
- Malaysia (250)
- Taiwan (300)

Latin / South America
- Mexico (500)
- Brazil (1,005)
- Chile (300)
- Colombia (300)

Europe
- United Kingdom (1,100)
- Germany (1,001)
- Spain (500)
- Austria (500)
- Switzerland (500)
- Romania (251)

Oceania
- Australia (1,021)
- New Zealand (567)

Unless otherwise noted, all data referenced in *The Connected Generation* were collected by Barna, among a nationally representative sample of the population identified. For this study, Barna relied on online collection methods, including mobile phone users.

The study used online national consumer panels that are representative by age, gender, region and ethnicity. Respondents were fully verified by the representative sample sources. Additionally, quality control measures checked that respondents were completing the survey at an appropriate pace and paying attention to the questions asked.

The survey was offered in nine different languages (English, French, Portuguese, Spanish, German, Romanian, Korean, Indonesian and Taiwanese), translated by a trusted translation service and verified by local partners in every country for context-specific nuance.

Based on the U.S. Census Bureau's International Data Base, the CIA World Fact Book and available census data from the U.S., Canada, Mexico, Chile, South Africa, Nigeria, Kenya, the UK, Germany, Spain, Austria, Switzerland, Romania, Australia, New Zealand, South Korea, India, Philippines and Singapore, quotas were designed to ensure the final group of adults interviewed in the study reflected each country's distribution of adults nationwide based on age, gender, ethnicity and region.

Online surveys necessitate literacy and an internet connection, which means the sample reflects adults who have those capabilities and does not reflect those who are unable to read or lack connectivity to respond to online surveys. Thus, in spite of a robust methodology, this sample is not meant to be representative of entire national populations, regions, continents or the world. The countries selected for this study were based on countries and regions where Barna and World Vision receive frequent requests for research-based insights. These and other concerns or limitations were respectfully considered while interpreting the data.

How to Use This Report

A Guide to *The Connected Generation*

One of many resources being produced from this groundbreaking research, *The Connected Generation* report is intended to offer Christian leaders an engaging overview of the findings about 18–35-year-olds around the world, particularly their perceptions and experiences with faith. Using various formats—data storytelling, original columns, expert Q&As, infographics and more—it has been packaged to suit a variety of reading and study experiences. The content is divided into three main sections, providing a glimpse into some specific facets of respondents' lives and building upon Barna's existing areas of research:

- **Life in an Anxious Age**: the milestones, relationships and emotions that mark respondents' early adulthood
- **Engagement with Spirituality & the Church**: openness to and affiliation with spirituality and religion at large, as well as how Christianity specifically is perceived, practiced and nurtured
- **Potential for Impact**: exploring 18–35-year-olds' desires to lead, find a calling and make a difference

At key points, essays from Barna president David Kinnaman expand upon the global findings and offer insights from his years spent studying and writing about the next generation.

In the Appendix, **Country Profiles** look at general religious attitudes and metrics for each country included in the study. Features such as **Country Comparisons** and **Connect the Dots** are scattered throughout to help readers and leaders make sense of the data in their context, and a **Glossary** defines terms that are foundational to Barna's reporting.

**Learn more at
theconnectedgeneration.com.**

Additional Resources from
The Connected Generation Project:

Country-specific reports, presenter slides and downloadable field guides

Extended interviews with expert contributors

The Faith for the Future webcast

Faith for Exiles by David Kinnaman and Mark Matlock

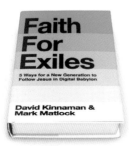

Who Are We Listening To?

It's important at the start of this report to acknowledge exactly who this study represents: respondents ages 18 to 35, from 25 different countries, who have an internet connection that allows them to participate in online surveys. The methodological obstacles make it difficult to conduct a study that is truly "global" this international sample, rather, includes a more literate, educated and urban population than would be wholly representative of all of these countries. This is important context to keep in mind, as even a study as extensive as this one has its limitations.

So how to refer to the 18–35-year-olds reported on here? Adults in this age range are sometimes called *Generation Y, Echo Boomers, iGen, Digital Natives* and so on. Barna has chosen to use a variety of other terms for them in these pages. First, for clarity, they are often referred to as 18–35-year-olds from around the world. This age group also bridges the generations Barna would typically cover as *Millennials* and *Gen Z*, labels you'll see occasionally in this report. The respondents may sometimes be referred to as *emerging generations, this generation* or *young adults*, the last of which we use to mean those on the lower end of the adult generations, not adolescents to whom this term is sometimes applied. Finally, for reasons that will become clear, we also proffer our own term: *the connected generation.*

COUNTRY COMPARISON

BEHIND THE NUMBERS

This report is based on a first-of-its-kind study that, in both scope and content, holds a unique place in Barna Group's 30+ years of research. This project involved not only a large and international sample but also an extensive and highly collaborative survey design process. Here's a peek at the numbers behind the data and how this portrait of the connected generation came to be.

TOTAL RESPONDENTS FROM EACH COUNTRY REPRESENTED

CANADA
1,000

UNITED STATES
2,000

MEXICO
500

COLOMBIA
300

BRAZIL
1,005

CHILE
300

The sample includes:

• **15,369** adults ages 18 to 35 in **25** countries

• **7,841** males and **7,479** females
  (49 "Other / Prefer not to respond")

9 language translations for the questionnaire, including English, French, Spanish, Portuguese, German, Romanian, Korean, Indonesian and Taiwanese

630 country-specific regions included in the questionnaire

94 country-specific levels of education included in the questionnaire

15 religious identity categories included in the questionnaire

144 ethnic and racial groups included in the questionnaire

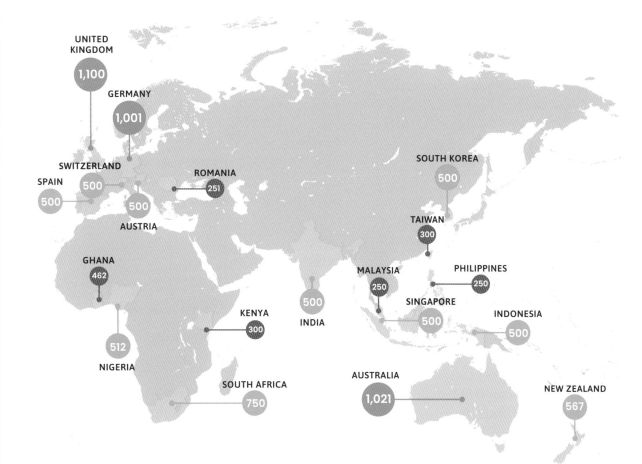

UNITED KINGDOM 1,100
GERMANY 1,001
SWITZERLAND 500
SPAIN 500
AUSTRIA 500
ROMANIA 251
SOUTH KOREA 500
TAIWAN 300
GHANA 462
MALAYSIA 250
PHILIPPINES 250
SINGAPORE 500
INDONESIA 500
KENYA 300
INDIA 500
NIGERIA 512
SOUTH AFRICA 750
AUSTRALIA 1,021
NEW ZEALAND 567

Glossary of Key Terms

Age Groups

Millennials are born between 1984 and 1998.

Gen Z are born between 1999 and 2015.

Education

For the purpose of international analysis, education level is split into three groupings, based on sample distribution in each country. The terms "bottom tier / least educated," "middle tier / average education" and "top tier / above average education" will be used to discuss education.

Connectivity Index

Individuals are ranked along a spectrum of connectivity according to how much they identify with eight factors across four categories of connection.

Globally connected:
Events around the world matter to me.
I feel connected to people around the world.

Relationally connected:
I often feel deeply cared for by those around me.
I often feel someone believes in me.

Forward-looking:
I often feel optimistic about the future.
I often feel able to accomplish my goals.

Outward-oriented:
What it takes to be an effective leader is changing.
Engage in four or more charitable activities (including giving, volunteering, advocating)

Strong connectivity: select 5–7 statements
Medium connectivity: select 3–4 statements
Weak connectivity: select 0–2 statements

Anxiety

Anxious respondents say they often feel at least three of the following four emotions: (1) anxious about important decisions; (2) sad or depressed; (3) afraid to fail and (4) insecure in who I am.

Faith Groups

Christians self-identify with a Christian denomination (Catholic, Protestant, Orthodox, "other").

Those of **other faiths** self-identify as Buddhist, Confucian, Hindu, Muslim, Jewish, Sikh, Taoist or "other."

Agnostic, atheists and nones self-identify as atheist or agnostic or do not identify with a religion.

Those who qualify as **practicing** members of Christianity or other faiths self-identify with that religion, attend a religious service other than a wedding or funeral at least once a month and say their faith is very important in their life.

Non-practicing members of Christianity or other faiths self-identify with that religion, attend a religious service other than a wedding or funeral a few times a year or less often and do not say that faith is very important in their life today.

Spiritual Categories of Those Who Experience Christianity

The following segments were originally defined and developed in research for David Kinnaman and Mark Matlock's book *Faith for Exiles* (Baker Books, 2019) and have been slightly adapted to apply to this international study of 18–35-year-olds.

> **Resilient disciples** are individuals who currently identify as Christian; attend church at least monthly and engage with their churches through more than just attendance; trust firmly in the authority of the Bible; are committed to Jesus personally and affirm he was crucified and raised from the dead to conquer sin and death; and express a desire to transform the broader society as an outcome of their faith.

Habitual churchgoers are individuals who currently identify as Christian and attend religious services other than weddings and funerals at least once a month yet do not meet the other requirements or hold the other foundational beliefs of resilient disciples.

Nomads (lapsed Christians) are individuals who currently identify as Christian but only attend religious services other than weddings or funerals once or twice a year at most.

Prodigals (ex-Christians) are individuals who do not currently identify as Christian despite having considered themselves to be a Christian in their upbringing.

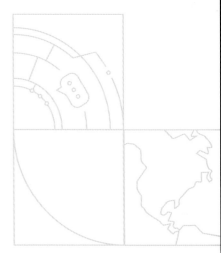

COUNTRY COMPARISON

RELIGIOUS CLIMATES

To understand how Christianity is perceived or practiced within specific atmospheres where it does or does not have cultural influence, countries included in this survey were grouped for analysis using a combination of historical trends, nationally representative secondary data and local partner input to determine their religious climate. *Though in most cases this categorization reflects the predominant religion of that nation, it is primarily an indication of the cultural or societal presence of the Christian faith.*

- **Secular** or post-Christian contexts are those in which Christianity and religion overall are on the decline, having less impact than they once did on politics and culture.
- **Christian** contexts are those where Christianity is either growing or has not seen a drastic decline in the past several generations; here, Christianity has an impact on culture and politics and is often identified as the societal norm.
- Finally, **Multi-faith** contexts are those that do not have a large Christian presence. In some of these contexts, a small Christian minority is growing.

The next page has country comparisons between nationally representative data and our 18–35-year-old respondents. These comparisons demonstrate both how this connected generation looks different than their countries as a whole and the changing context young adults are living in.

Secular climate   Christian climate   ● Multi-faith climate

RELIGIOUS AFFILIATION, BY RELIGIOUS CLIMATE

● Identify as Christian ● Identify with other faiths ● Identify with no faith

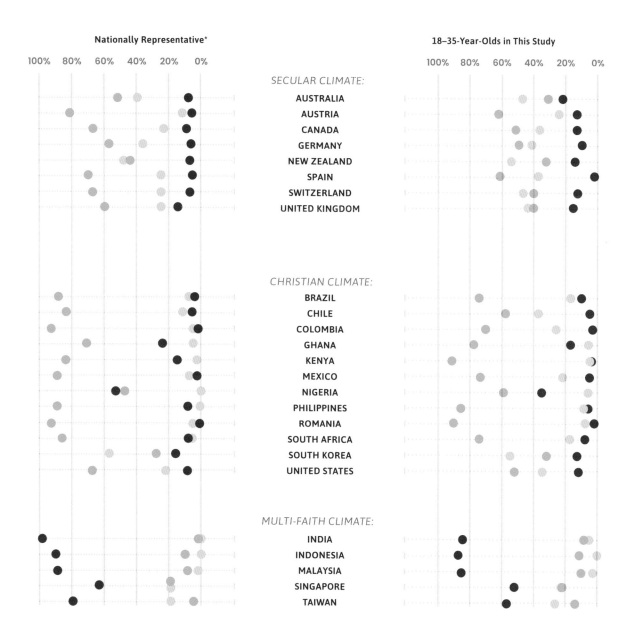

Nationally Representative*

100% 80% 60% 40% 20% 0%

18–35-Year-Olds in This Study

100% 80% 60% 40% 20% 0%

SECULAR CLIMATE:
AUSTRALIA
AUSTRIA
CANADA
GERMANY
NEW ZEALAND
SPAIN
SWITZERLAND
UNITED KINGDOM

CHRISTIAN CLIMATE:
BRAZIL
CHILE
COLOMBIA
GHANA
KENYA
MEXICO
NIGERIA
PHILIPPINES
ROMANIA
SOUTH AFRICA
SOUTH KOREA
UNITED STATES

MULTI-FAITH CLIMATE:
INDIA
INDONESIA
MALAYSIA
SINGAPORE
TAIWAN

*Source: CIA World Fact Book • n=15,369 adults ages 18 to 35, December 4, 2018–February 15, 2019.

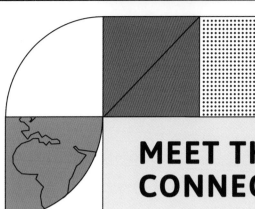

MEET THE CONNECTED GENERATION

Connected but Alone
Despite being a hyper-connected and globally minded generation, many young adults say they feel lonely.

Spiritual Openness
There is a general (and, at times, surprising) openness toward spirituality, religion and, in many cases, the Church—but less so among those who have left their faith.

Age of Anxiety
Worry and insecurity, often tied to finances and vocation, are prominent traits among a generation that has come of age in a chaotic, complex time.

Looking at the general state of faith & well-being among 18–35-year-olds around the world, these are the stories that stand out

Looking for Answers
Human suffering and global conflict are among the top issues that raise spiritual doubts for 18–35-year-olds.

Resilient Discipleship
Across religious climates, the data point to keys for forming faithful Christ-followers, even among those Christians who lapse in religiosity.

Longing to Make a Difference
When young adults engage with a community of worship, they're looking for concrete teaching, opportunities to fight injustice and friends to join them along the way.

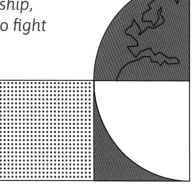

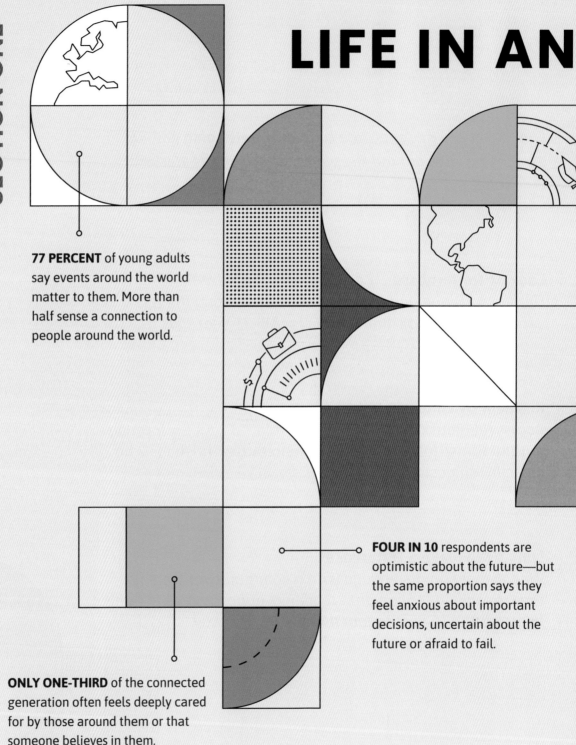

LIFE IN AN

77 PERCENT of young adults say events around the world matter to them. More than half sense a connection to people around the world.

FOUR IN 10 respondents are optimistic about the future—but the same proportion says they feel anxious about important decisions, uncertain about the future or afraid to fail.

ONLY ONE-THIRD of the connected generation often feels deeply cared for by those around them or that someone believes in them.

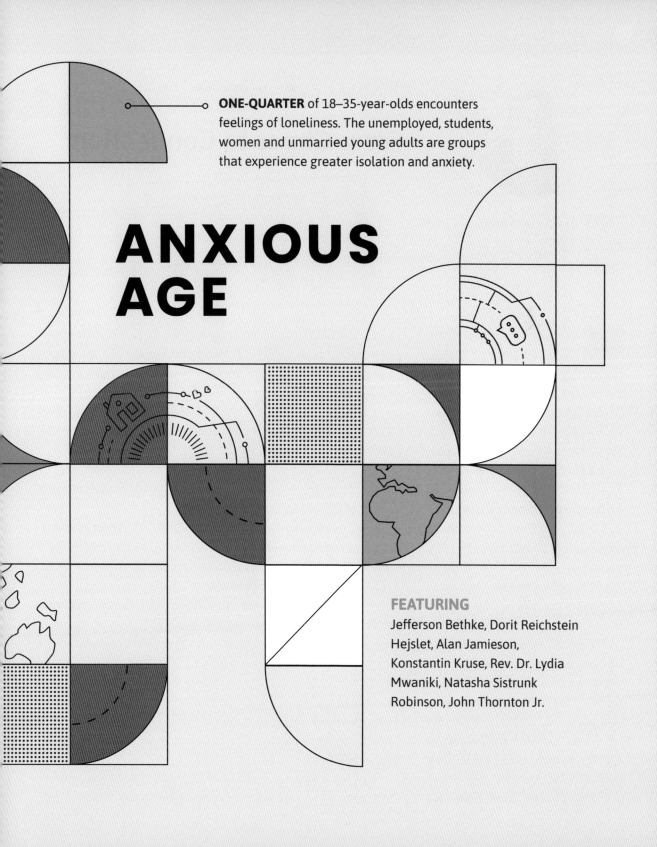

ONE-QUARTER of 18–35-year-olds encounters feelings of loneliness. The unemployed, students, women and unmarried young adults are groups that experience greater isolation and anxiety.

ANXIOUS AGE

FEATURING

Jefferson Bethke, Dorit Reichstein Hejslet, Alan Jamieson, Konstantin Kruse, Rev. Dr. Lydia Mwaniki, Natasha Sistrunk Robinson, John Thornton Jr.

DAVID KINNAMAN
President at Barna Group
UNITED STATES

From Chaos to Connection

BY DAVID KINNAMAN
with contributions from Daniel Copeland,
Aly Hawkins & Alyce Youngblood

F or years now, our team has gone to great lengths to listen to the stories and experiences of teenagers and young adults across the religious spectrum—from devoted Christ followers to ex-Christians, from passionate adherents of other faiths to those for whom religion is an artifact of a bygone era. Over a decade and a half, we've been privileged to interview nearly 100,000 young people. We've been interested in every aspect of their lives, trying to put the scraps of evidence together to form a coherent picture for Christian leaders to understand and respond to.

I've written three books based on what we've heard that help to address the spiritual journeys of young adults: ***unChristian*** (2007), which asks, *What does Christianity look like to young non-Christians?*; ***You Lost Me*** (2011), which asks, *Why do young adults walk away from church and from faith?*; and ***Faith for Exiles*** (2019), which asks, *What practices distinguish resilient disciples among young Christians?*

Through our careful listening, we've come to hold several core convictions about these young adult generations, whom we call Millennials and Gen Z:

- They are deeply misunderstood by older generations of Christian leaders.
- They are coming of age in a radically different context, one that could be defined as chaotic, as we'll describe.
- Their skepticism is giving way to indifference—a much more intractable problem.
- The challenges and opportunities of discipleship are more complex.
- They are hungry to see courageous leaders in all facets of society.

This is a generation of contrast, of contradiction. As one example, they are more connected than ever before, yet their connectivity coexists with paradoxical levels of isolation and loneliness.

The book you are reading is both the latest—and by far the largest—installment in Barna's effort to understand the contours of faith and faithfulness among young adults. In partnership with our friends at World Vision, this is our first-ever global look at 18–35-year-olds. The data we've collected falls naturally into three big domains:

- **Life in an Anxious Age:** What is the broader context of this generation—the cultural, demographic and social trends shaping their world?

- *Engagement with Spirituality & the Church:* How do they affiliate with (if at all) and what do they believe about spirituality and religion? How do they perceive Christianity? What factors are growing faith and influencing church engagement?

- *Potential for Impact:* Where and how are they being shaped to lead? What do they care about and what motivates them to do things in their communities?

Here at the outset, I want to acknowledge the Barna team's perspectives and limitations as English-speaking, (primarily) culturally American, joyfully Christian researchers, analysts and leaders. This recognition brings with it a heaping dose of humility. We are keenly aware that the insights offered in this report are informed by, and sometimes alloyed with, our cultural values, allegiances and assumptions. Still, we believe the data we have gathered presents other social observers, data interpreters, trend watchers and ministry practitioners from different backgrounds and in different places with an unprecedented invitation to *listen*—and then to respond in ways that will strengthen the global-yet-always-local Church.

Consider this: We've done *more than 8,000 hours* of interviews with young adults across the globe, eager to share their views and experiences with someone who will listen. And,

WE MUST SLOW DOWN AND LISTEN TO A GENERATION THAT IS TOO OFTEN TALKED AT AND TALKED ABOUT

as my daughter Annika reminds me, *behind every survey is a story.* A story of hope and opportunity. Maybe a story of financial insecurity and anxiety about the future, or of abuse and marginalization. A story of spiritual renewal and thriving community.

Are we listening?

To be effective leaders—of churches, businesses, cultural organizations, government agencies, development NGOs, political movements, *whatever*—we must slow down and listen to a generation that is too often talked *at* and talked *about*. We must stop ignoring or dismissing or rolling our eyes at teens, twentysomethings and thirtysomethings who are coming into their own. They are desperately in need of a wise, compassionate, listening ear—

and we are desperately in need of their partnership as we look to the Church's future.

Our Chaotic Moment

I was in Honduras last spring with Annika and my son, Zack. One of our day trips was a visit to coffee fields high in the mountains, where we met local farmers and had a chance to learn about their day-to-day lives. I was surprised and then amused to hear one man's complaint, echoed by several colleagues, about neighbors going to great lengths to obtain his Wi-Fi password so they could watch YouTube. Even at a remote elevation in Central America, YouTube is linking emerging generations to a bigger, broader world!

Technologies that enable young adults to be the most connected generation in human history—to world events, to others' suffering, to products and services and ideas from anywhere and everywhere, to each other—are disrupting the contexts in which coming of age and passing on faith have traditionally taken place. Many teens and young adults, knowingly or not, are trading family- and community-curated knowledge for information managed by market-based algorithms. The average so-

cial media user sees only what a computer calculation determines they should see, based on their consumer potential. Users who post the most get the most attention, and those who get the most attention are favored by the algorithm.

Not the wisest. Not the most life-giving or humane. Not the most peacemaking. Not the most Kingdom-minded.

The outcome, all too often, is social and cultural commodification, polarization and—ironically—*dis*connection.[1]

My friend Mark Sayers, who does more than his fair share of listening, contends that our current moment is characterized by five trends that have thrown our world into chaos:

1. *Radical Connectivity:* New technology is bringing us closer together while tearing us apart.
2. *Competing Visions*: From a global village to a confusing, conflicted bazaar of ideas.
3. *Faltering Secular Revival*: We are becoming less religious and more religious at the same time.
4. *Deep Hunger for a Better World*: There is a growing gap between elites and the public, the haves and have-nots.
5. *The Great Disillusionment*: Our foundations of meaning, our stories, patterns and institutions, are fracturing under intense pressure.[2]

His ideas have a lot in common with what I've come to call "digital Babylon," the pagan-but-spiritual, hyperstimulated, multicultural, imperial crossroads that is the virtual home of every person with Wi-Fi or a mobile data plan (or, for many of us, both).[3] As in ancient Babylon, living as exiles in digital Babylon stretches and strains the people of God, by turns corrupting and refining as we wrestle with how to be faithful and remain resilient in this strange land.

Radical Connectivity

Long before I'd heard Mark Sayers talk about his five trends, the Barna team began to analyze the mountain of data that was coming in from 18–35-year-olds worldwide. An early and obvious theme to emerge was broad agreement with two statements: "Events around the world matter to me" (77% all) and "I feel connected to people around the world" (57%). Since so many teens and young adults from diverse coun-tries and cultures appeared to share a sense of global connected-ness, we hypothesized this might serve as a lens through which we could bring them into clearer fo-cus. We thus began to develop a "connectivity index," based on a series of eight factors in four cat-egories that speak to the unique risks and potential rewards pre-sented to this generation. Each factor concerns a different aspect of how a person perceives he or she is connected to the world.

Let's take stock of those four dimensions for a minute. Do you

CATEGORIES OF CONNECTIVITY

GLOBAL

1. "Events around the world matter to me" 77%

2. "I feel connected to people around the world" 57%

RELATIONAL

3. "I often feel deeply cared for by those around me" 33%

4. "I often feel someone believes in me" 32%

FORWARD-LOOKING

5. "I often feel optimistic about the future" 40%

6. "I often feel able to accomplish my goals" 34%

OUTWARD-ORIENTED

7. "What it takes to be an effective leader is changing" 29%

8. Engage in four or more charitable activities* 30%

n=15,369 adults ages 18 to 35, December 4, 2018–February 15, 2019.
*including donating, volunteering and advocating

THE VAST MAJORITY OF THE CONNECTED GENERATION FEELS THE IMPACT OF BROAD, GLOBAL TRENDS MORE THAN THEY FEEL LOVED AND SUPPORTED BY OTHERS CLOSE TO THEM

see the one factor that triggers the highest response? Global connectivity. The dimensions we measured for global connection far outpace other aspects of connectedness assessed in the study. "Events around the world" and "people around the world" surface more frequently than any of the other three areas of connection: relational, forward-looking and outward-oriented. This suggests that the vast majority of the connected generation feels the impact of broad, global trends *more than* they feel loved and supported by others close to them, *more than* they feel optimistic and empowered, *more than* they express an outward orientation to change and personal activism.

We also discovered a lot of good news; many young adults are thriving in unexpected ways, so don't let these stats paint the generation with too unflattering a shade. However, the paradox of a connected-but-disconnected generation is clear:

- ***Despite being digital natives, relational connection is lacking for most young adults.*** Only one-third of the connected generation (33%) says they "often feel deeply cared for by those around me." The same proportion (32%) indicates that "someone believes in me."

- ***Despite living in a time of relative peace and social mobility,* most young adults are not optimistic or empowered about their future***. Just two out of five (40%) claim to be optimistic about the future and only one-third (34%) says they often feel able to accomplish their goals.

- ***Although this generation is rightly concerned about justice causes and healthy expressions of leadership, they often lack personal engagement in the solutions they desire.*** Just one-third participates in an above average-amount of charitable activities (including giving, volunteering or advocating) for causes they care about, and three in 10 say they believe that what it takes to be an effective leader is changing.

In other words, the world feels bigger, more unpredictable, more immediate and more risky. At the same time, young adults' personal relationships, their agency to influence the future and their positive engagement with society are not always a reliable resource for these young people.

All of this adds up to a world that feels in flux. Up for grabs. Chaotic.

Clusters of Connectivity

Because we are geeks, and we like to make clusters to analyze, we grouped our 15,000+ respondents into three segments based on the number of eight connectivity factors they met. We wanted to see if certain young adults feel more connected than others.

*Of course, this is not true for every country or context today, but the global upheaval that faced the World War 2 generation or the remaking of global order under the Baby Boomers are examples of less-stable global settings that influenced previous generations.

The results look like this: About one-quarter (23%) meets five or more of the eight factors and thus qualifies as having strong connectivity. Tens of millions of 18–35-year-olds around the world seem to exhibit positive connections in the four areas we assessed—that's good news! The second group is the largest, but only by a small margin: 39 percent of young adults meet three or four of the eight indicators, which qualifies them as having medium connectivity.

The final group has two or fewer of the connectivity flags, representing nearly two out of every five young adults (38%). That is, nearly two out of five young adults globally are dealing with weak levels of connection. Their relational connections, in particular, tend to struggle: Fewer than one in 10 in this segment says they have someone in their life who believes in them.

Grouping young adults according to their sense of connectivity allows us to take a closer look at what characteristics and experiences, if any, they have in common with others who show similarly strong or weak connectivity. After iso-

NEARLY TWO OUT OF FIVE YOUNG ADULTS GLOBALLY ARE DEALING WITH WEAK LEVELS OF CONNECTION

lating various demographics and running statistical regressions (I told you we love to geek out), our team found two areas that are highly correlated with young adults' sense of connectivity: their *faith commitment* and their *perception of financial security*. Millennials and Gen Z are more likely to express strong connectivity on the eight dimensions if they are a practicing Christian (see definitions on page 12) and / or when they feel financially stable, and more likely to exhibit weak connectivity if they do not practice any faith and / or when feeling economically insecure.

I want to underscore this good news: Strong levels of connectiv-

CONNECTIVITY INDEX

23% Strong connectivity (meets 5 to 8 factors)

39% Medium connectivity (meets 3 to 4 factors)

38% Weak connectivity (meets 0 to 2 factors)

n=15,369 adults ages 18 to 35, December 4, 2018–February 15, 2019.

ity are associated with faith in general and with Christianity in particular. Note that it's not just calling oneself a Christian, but actually practicing the faith that makes such a difference. (There's even stronger connectivity among a group we call resilient disciples, as we'll see on page 95.)

When it comes to the other fac-tor, financial security, a person's experience of economic stability or instability isn't about their actual income—or, at least, not entirely. People with weak connectivity are more likely than average to say they are unemployed, to fall in the bottom third of their country's average educational attain-ment and to be divorced or separated (all of which can have a negative relationship to stability). They are also more likely than young adults with medium or strong connectivity to say they often feel "unable to do what I want" (33% vs. 26% medium, 18% strong), "uncertain about the future" (48%

CONNECTIVITY, BY FAITH PRACTICE

● Strong connectivity ● Medium connectivity ● Weak connectivity

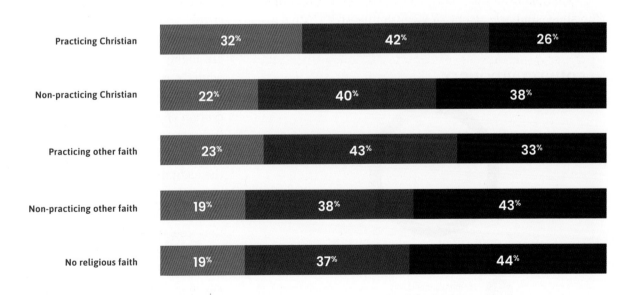

	Strong	Medium	Weak
Practicing Christian	32%	42%	26%
Non-practicing Christian	22%	40%	38%
Practicing other faith	23%	43%	33%
Non-practicing other faith	19%	38%	43%
No religious faith	19%	37%	44%

n=15,369 adults ages 18 to 35, December 4, 2018–February 15, 2019.

vs. 38%, 30%) and that "there are not enough opportunities available to me" (25% vs. 23%, 19%). Feelings of security emanate from a constellation of experiences and relational connections, not just from literal money in the bank.

Meet the Connected Generation

We call them "the connected generation" because we are listening. And what they are telling us, among many other valuable things, is that being and feeling connected helps to define them.[4]

As we show you what we're hearing from young people and leaders from around the world, our prayer is that you will listen, too. Some of the precious people whom this data represents are filled with hope. Others, as you'll see, are deeply hurting. Churches, ministries and parents who hope to make disciples who pass on their faith to future generations must listen first.

As you dive into this report, you'll learn more about how 18–35-year-olds are positioned—with regard to their families, communities, careers and personal well-being—in an era of disruption. And, as you come to better understand the culture they inhabit, you'll be better prepared to help them reframe their chaotic experience into strong connection. ⬤

STRONG LEVELS OF CONNECTIVITY ARE ASSOCIATED WITH FAITH IN GENERAL AND WITH CHRISTIANITY IN PARTICULAR

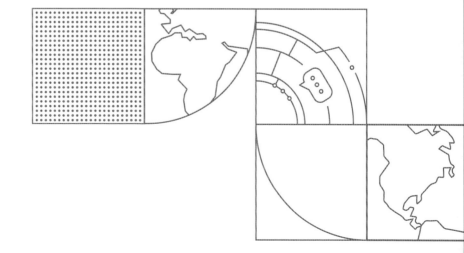

THE CONNECTIVITY SPECTRUM

A DATA PROFILE OF YOUNG ADULTS WITH THE STRONGEST AND WEAKEST LEVELS OF CONNECTION

WHICH GROUPS ARE MORE LIKELY TO HAVE *WEAK* CONNECTIVITY?

43%	42%	48%	45%	49%	42%	44%
Rural	Bottom third of education	Unemployed	Struggling financially	Divorced / separated	Secular religious climate	Atheist / agnostic / none

CONNECTION COMPARISONS

The strength or weakness of a young person's connectivity correlates with a host of other activities, perceptions and attitudes. All in all, those with stronger connectivity have a deeper experience of well-being—spiritually and otherwise—while those with weaker connectivity are struggling.

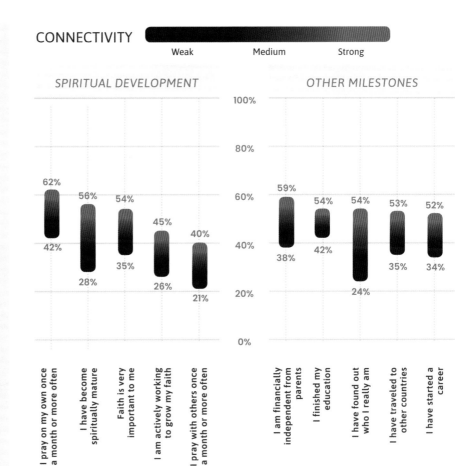

CONNECTIVITY

Weak · Medium · Strong

SPIRITUAL DEVELOPMENT

	Weak	Strong
I pray on my own once a month or more often	42%	62%
I have become spiritually mature	28%	56%
Faith is very important to me	35%	54%
I am actively working to grow my faith	26%	45%
I pray with others once a month or more often	21%	40%

OTHER MILESTONES

	Weak	Strong
I am financially independent from parents	38%	59%
I finished my education	42%	54%
I have found out who I really am	24%	54%
I have traveled to other countries	35%	53%
I have started a career	34%	52%

Barna created a custom index to assess Millennial and Gen Z young adults' level of personal connection to world events, to people around them, to the future and to making a difference (see page 23 for details on how analysts designed these categories of connectivity).

WHICH GROUPS ARE MORE LIKELY TO HAVE *STRONG CONNECTIVITY*?

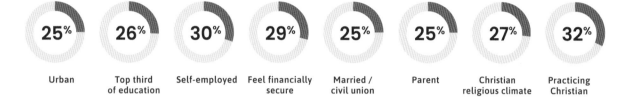

25%	26%	30%	29%	25%	25%	27%	32%
Urban	Top third of education	Self-employed	Feel financially secure	Married / civil union	Parent	Christian religious climate	Practicing Christian

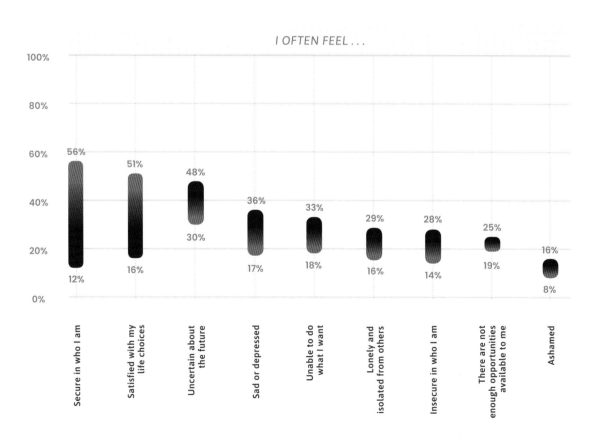

I OFTEN FEEL . . .

- Secure in who I am — 56% / 12%
- Satisfied with my life choices — 51% / 16%
- Uncertain about the future — 48% / 30%
- Sad or depressed — 36% / 17%
- Unable to do what I want — 33% / 18%
- Lonely and isolated from others — 29% / 16%
- Insecure in who I am — 28% / 14%
- There are not enough opportunities available to me — 25% / 19%
- Ashamed — 16% / 8%

n=15,369 adults ages 18 to 35, December 4, 2018–February 15, 2019.

COUNTRY COMPARISON

CONNECTIVITY LEVELS AROUND THE WORLD

● Strong connectivity   ● Medium connectivity   ● Weak connectivity

AUSTRALIA	AUSTRIA	BRAZIL	CANADA	CHILE
● 20%	● 21%	● 26%	● 25%	● 37%
● 39%	● 40%	● 41%	● 37%	● 43%
● 40%	● 38%	● 33%	● 39%	● 20%

COLOMBIA	GERMANY	GHANA	INDIA	INDONESIA
● 37%	● 18%	● 30%	● 21%	● 22%
● 39%	● 38%	● 39%	● 46%	● 40%
● 24%	● 44%	● 31%	● 33%	● 38%

KENYA	MALAYSIA	MEXICO	NEW ZEALAND	NIGERIA
● 36%	● 15%	● 28%	● 22%	● 32%
● 40%	● 40%	● 46%	● 35%	● 42%
● 24%	● 46%	● 26%	● 43%	● 25%

PHILIPPINES	ROMANIA	SINGAPORE	SOUTH AFRICA	SOUTH KOREA
● 29%	● 19%	● 15%	● 29%	● 12%
● 48%	● 47%	● 38%	● 41%	● 28%
● 24%	● 34%	● 46%	● 31%	● 60%

SPAIN	SWITZERLAND	TAIWAN	UNITED KINGDOM	UNITED STATES
● 24%	● 22%	● 14%	● 12%	● 23%
● 44%	● 38%	● 35%	● 38%	● 38%
● 32%	● 40%	● 51%	● 50%	● 38%

n=15,369 adults ages 18 to 35, December 4, 2018–February 15, 2019.

Family Benefits

MARRIAGE AND PARENTING—OFTEN TIED TO FAITH
AND SECURITY—AREN'T YET THE NORM FOR YOUNG
ADULTS

Much has been made of Millennials, especially in Western contexts, postponing marriage and parenthood, often in favor of pursuing education, new cities, home ownership, professional stability or other personal experiences like travel.[5] Looking at this study's sample of 18–35-year-olds, we generally see this trend bearing out around the world.

Just over one-quarter (27%) is married, and just over one-third (35%) is a parent. Though reports of having children usually accompany reports of being married, one in five single young adults in this study (19%) is a parent. *Movements toward marriage and parenting tend to run parallel, with the late 20s and early 30s being the turning point for starting a family.* Naturally, those on the younger end of this age spectrum are less likely to have a spouse or child: Among those under age 25, 7 percent are married and 14 percent are parents; among those ages 25 to 30, rates of marriage climb to 30 percent and parenting to 39 percent. Past age 30, having a spouse (50%) or child (60%) becomes more commonplace.

Religious Young Adults Are More Likely to Have Started Families

A main predictor of relationship and family status is faith. *The closer one is to religion, the earlier they get married or have children.* This is true for Christians (30% married, 40% parents) as well as those who identify with other religions (32% married, 33% parents) when compared to atheists, agnostics and those of no faith (18% married, 28% parents). The life cycle of faith is correlated with the likelihood of being married, with young adults who have always been religious (31%) leading in rates of marriage (vs. 25% of those who became religious, 21% of those who left religion and 16% of those who have never been religious).

Religious young adults who are already married or raising children may be spurred by their values or by the traditions or expectations of their religious culture. In addition, starting a family may spur a deeper engagement in faith. From either direction, *there is a link between family and faith.*

As Milestones Pass, Security Grows

Family-related milestones are wrapped up with, and may often follow, achievements outside the home, such as education and employment. For example, very few students are married (4%), while one-third of those in the workplace (32%) and 39 percent of those in the top tier of education have gotten married. Granted, as a result of where and how this online international survey was conducted, the sample reflects greater than average education and resources. This is important socioeconomic context to keep in mind in interpreting respondents'

HOW MARITAL & FAMILY STATUS RELATE TO STABILITY

● Married   ● Unmarried   ● Parents   ● Not parents

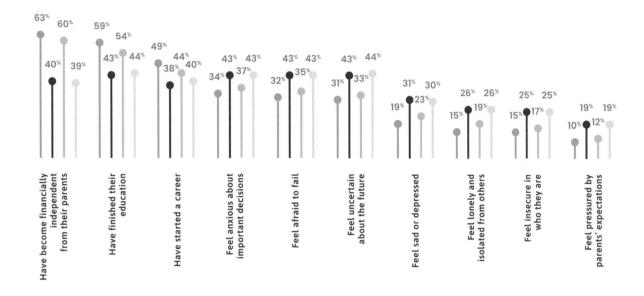

n=15,369 adults ages 18 to 35, December 4, 2018–February 15, 2019.

decisions surrounding education, career, marriage and family—starting with the acknowledgment that they may have more decisions available to them in the first place.

Respondents who indicate having already become a spouse or parent are more likely to say they have also completed their education, become financially independent, started a career or purchased a home. One might think compounded responsibility means added stress, but **_tipping points in life stage seem to be accompanied by positive emotional states._** Generally, those who are married or have children report optimism, satisfaction and security and are less often burdened by anxieties. Meanwhile, young adults without these personal family bonds, especially those without a spouse, are in a more precarious emotional position and are significantly more likely to report feelings of

isolation, insecurity, sadness or depression. (However, there are some gendered nuances to this story, as reported on page 42.)

For church leaders, these findings should raise questions about how to connect with 18–35-year-olds who haven't started families—a group who, remember, tend to be younger, in a season of professional or economic uncertainty, and less religious. What support might they need as they establish themselves in community, career and—maybe someday—family? ●

Meet the Millennial Parents

WHAT WE KNOW ABOUT THE MINORITY OF
18–35-YEAR-OLDS WHO ARE ALREADY RAISING A
NEW GENERATION

Who exactly are the 35 percent of young adults who, unlike the majority of their peers, have not delayed having children? Barna wanted to know more about this segment—who represent a growing minority of their generation, a counter to many stereotypes about young adults' delayed adolescence and a fresh area of research. Here, we'll take a look at what matters most to these parents, how they are faring in this season of child-rearing and what they want from the future.

The Different Experiences of Single Parents & Married Parents

Young adults who are parents differ from their generation overall—and at times from one another—in key ways. The first is, perhaps, expected: Most of them are married. Sixty percent of 18–35-year-olds who have children also presently have a spouse. Another one in five is unmarried but in some form of committed partnership. A small minority of these young parents has previously been married, though 16 percent identify as single and never married. Overall, one in five respondents in this study has both a spouse and child(ren), while 14 percent are unmarried parents.

The emotional state of parents in this connected generation is correlated with marital status. Though parents in this study overall appear more emotionally secure than their non-parent peers (see page 32), the concerns and mental well-being of unmarried parents more closely mirror that of non-parents. Unmarried parents in this study are much more likely than married parents to feel lonely and isolated (25% vs. 14%) or depressed and sad (31% vs. 17%). Lacking some relational support and usually on the younger end of the age spectrum, unmarried parents are also more likely to experience other stressors—including pressure from their own parents.

Parents Prioritize Faithfulness —for Their Children

Generally, faith is a priority for these parents, more so than for their peers without children. More than four in 10 parents in this generation (42%) strongly agree their religious faith is very important in their life; less than one-third of young adults who aren't parents (31%) says the same. Accordingly, nearly one-third of respondents who are not parents (32%) is agnostic, atheist or otherwise irreligious, while 77 percent of parents identify with a religion.

For many, these religious values have been with them since their own youth. One-third of young parents who were religious growing up (33%) says they were "very active" in their faith as teenagers.

Parents in this age group also tend to be serious about practicing their faith today, particularly when compared to members of their generation who don't have children. On a monthly basis, nearly three in five parents (58%) in this study pray on their own (vs. 51% overall), and more than one-third (35%) prays with others (vs. 29%). Young parents are also much more likely to read scripture compared to their non-parent peers (29% versus 22%, respectively). Naturally, these percentages rise among Christian parents (74% pray on their own, 45% pray with others, 40% read scripture privately).

Interestingly, of those who say they are part of a faith group, there is no statistical variation in weekly worship community attendance among religious parents

DORIT REICHSTEIN HEJSLET
Communications for Open Doors Denmark, mother to three children
DENMARK

KONSTANTIN KRUSE
Pastor, father to two children
GERMANY

In Their Words: Parents' Perspectives

Do you think the approach of parents in your age group will be different from that of previous generations?
DORIT: We are scrutinized every day in the media about what we should and should not do in order not to screw up our kids. We are told that we as parents are solely responsible for our children's mental and physical well-being, and we have to be almost perfect. There is a lot of shaming toward parents today. I have a hard time relaxing. I am constantly focused on doing my very best and that sometimes makes me a worried, anxious parent.

Do you feel different from non-parents in your generation?
KONSTANTIN: Many of my closest friends are also in my generation and have kids. I think differences between parents and non-parents in my generation are the differences in the amount of responsibility. When you have kids you spend your time, energy and money differently. Parents are also typically not as flexible with the schedule as perhaps those without kids.

How has the responsibility of being a parent affected your faith practice?
KONSTANTIN: The hope is that they see what a natural and authentic relationship with Jesus looks like—whether it is serving the community, leading in church or how I love my family. I understand that it starts with me being an example for my family so that they can see what it looks like to serve the Lord—and through this example they will then hopefully also know and serve him.

DORIT: It is so much harder to focus on singing, praying or listening to the sermon with kids at church. To be touched by the Word and the Spirit is hard because I am constantly interrupted. I have to give a word of encouragement to a fellow church member with my baby on my hip. It might not feel very holy or like it used to, but it is my kind of discipline and spiritual devotion, and I think God knows how devoted it really is.

(continued on next page)

(continued …)

As you think about the next 10 years, what would you like to see happen in your life?

DORIT: We are renovating an old house. It's our dream to see this turn into a home and a base for us and our children. I want to bless others through our home. I want to settle in the town where we moved and plant deep roots, show love to this city, serve my neighborhood by showing them Jesus and his love.

KONSTANTIN: In the next 10 years, I would like to support my wife in her calling and would love to see my kids loving Jesus and see the Church thriving. Personally, I would love to become a better leader and do my best to help others find their own purpose and calling in ministry.

and non-parents. Among their motivations for attendance, however, there is one significant difference: More than one-third of attending religious young parents (35%) says they participate in their place of worship "for their children." This reason is the third most common motivation among parents, just behind personal spiritual priorities of learning about God or growing in faith. This suggests that, though faithful respondents are fairly consistent in their religious service attendance regardless of their family arrangement, their reasons for consistency shift after having children. This study also speaks to the reality that many adults may become more committed to church if children enter the picture; among respondents who have some connection to Christianity, 38 percent of those who aren't parents assume they will become more involved in church if they have kids.

What's Next for Young Parents?

As you can see, parents in this study—typically married, established in career and financially independent—have hit some tangible milestones in their lives thus far; looking forward, nearly half (45%) now have their eyes on owning a home. But other hopes they hold for the next 10 years are much like the hopes of any 18–35-year-old. Like their non-

PARENTS IN THIS STUDY

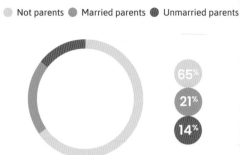

Not parents   Married parents   Unmarried parents

65%
21%
14%

n=15,369 adults ages 18 to 35, December 4, 2018–February 15, 2019.

parent peers, 37 percent of parents in this study want to follow their dreams (vs. 39% of those who aren't parents). One-fifth (21%) wants to find out who they really are (vs. 25%). These parents also share their generation's desire to travel (31% vs. 33%), help the poor (24% vs. 22%) and mature spiritually (20% vs. 21%) in the coming decade. They also believe and behave similarly to the average young adult when it comes to humanitarian responsibility, concerns about the world or experiences of church.

For churches trying to minister to—and with—this generation, it's important to remember the ways in which this driven group of parents are both unique and similar to their peers. Ultimately, churches aren't just walking alongside the few parents in this generation, but also helping disciple the children to whom they are already passing down their faith. ◉

Working Order

YOUNG ADULTS' IDENTITY, ACHIEVEMENTS AND
EMOTIONS CENTER AROUND CAREER

Much of Barna's research in the U.S. has pointed to an urgency surrounding career—and thus a need for vocational discipleship (see page 120)—among Millennials and Gen Z, and this study underscores these themes on an international level. When asked to reflect on what they've accomplished in life so far, 18–35-year-olds' top responses reveal that *the priority of their early adulthood has been establishing themselves financially and professionally.* About half say they have "completed their education" (48%) or "become financially independent from their parents" (46%). Four in 10 (41%) mention "starting their career," and 15 percent have gone so far as "starting their own business" (see sidebar for more about these entrepreneurial members of this generation). Nearly one-third (31%) says they have "followed their dreams," an effort that may be tangential to some of these more explicitly professional achievements.

These milestones are more commonly reported than ones related to family, such as "getting married" (25%) or "having children" (31%). The minority who is already married or raising children, however, is more likely to claim other markers of pro-

fessional and financial stability too. Though this study does not speak to the order of such events, 18–35-year-olds who have started families also have higher levels of education and employment (see page 32). Overall, respondents seem to plot the journey into adulthood along a linear path, one that moves first through the classroom and / or the workplace before moving toward the home. In fact, thinking about the next 10 years of their lives and what they'd like to achieve, young adults generally worry more about buying a home (53%) than about the family who might fill it (41% would like to get married, 33% would like to have children in the next decade).

Naturally, there is some relationship between education and employment: Those in the top tier of education are more likely to be working (84% vs. 76% of the middle tier, 55% of the bottom tier), though one in five students in this sample says they do work in some capacity (5% full-time, 16% part-time). Men are more likely than women to be employed, and respondents who live in urban or suburban environments have greater rates of employment than peers in rural or small town settings.

Students & Unemployed Young Adults Struggle with Insecurity

There are significant emotional patterns tied to the learning and working lives of young adults.

EMOTIONS & EMPLOYMENT

"I often feel ..."

All working   All unemployed   Students   Entrepreneurs

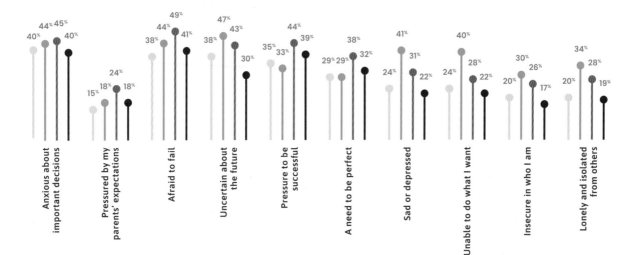

n=15,369 adults ages 18 to 35, December 4, 2018–February 15, 2019.

Eighteen–35-year-olds who are students or unemployed tend to express feelings of anxiety or hopelessness, while ***positive emotions are correlated with being gainfully employed.***

The unemployed are less likely to feel able to accomplish their goals (24% vs. 36% of all working 18–35-year-olds), satisfied with their life choices (22% vs. 32%) or secure in who they are (21% vs. 31%). Meanwhile, they express more uncertainty about the future (47% vs. 38%) and feel they are unable to do what they want

(40% vs. 24%) or that there are not enough opportunities available to them (32% vs. 21%). Given this, it's not surprising that four in 10 unemployed young adults (41% vs. 24%) say they are sad or depressed, and one-third (34% vs. 20%) feels lonely. Students in particular sense pressure to be successful (45% vs. 35% of all working 18–35-year-olds), a need to be perfect (38% vs. 29%) and high expectations from parents (24% vs. 15%). Half of students (49% vs. 38%) are contending with a fear of failure.

There are a number of factors that might contribute to this reported insecurity among those who aren't (yet) succeeding in career. For example, students are often on the younger end of the age spectrum for this study and facing a lot of unknowns, usually without the familial support that may come from having a spouse and / or children. In addition, young adults who aren't working may feel the stress of financial burdens. But there are broader issues related to identity and community implied in the apparent vulnerability among this generation—and beyond them. At least in the United States, today's teenagers may be even more likely to define themselves primarily by their professional and academic achievements, Barna research suggests.[6]

Whatever their phase of career or level of employment, *18- to 35-year-olds are navigating new professional terrain.* More than a fad, a freelancer and gig economy is encountering growing pains—among them, irregular income, which a global PayPal study indicates is a significant problem in Southeast Asia.[7] Flexible and remote work options, despite their popularity and convenience, can be accompanied by loneliness and burnout.[8] And, all the while, young adults in many nations also face staggering student debt conditions.[9]

Career-building, in general and in this era, comes with sharply felt benefits and burdens. Thus, work emerges as a core focus for the young adults in this survey—and, likewise, should be an emphasis for churches hoping to engage with this driven generation. ●

The Personal & Spiritual Maturity of Young Entrepreneurs

The minority of 18–35-year-olds who say they have started a business reports high levels of achievement or experience across many other realms of life, from starting families to traveling the world. A lot of their hard work appears to have occurred internally, and signs of faith and fortitude line the ambitious path of entrepreneurialism. Though this study can't speak specifically to their success, these young adults are more likely than their non-entrepreneurial peers to say they have followed their dreams (49% vs. 28%) or found out who they really are (45% vs. 34%). For the most part, they express more positive emotions, though they are similar to young adults who have not started their own businesses in their levels of anxiety over big decisions (40% and 41%) or fear of failure (41% and 40%). A particularly religious group—six in 10 (59% vs. 40% overall) say faith is very important to them—they are also inclined to say they have become spiritually mature (52% vs. 38% of non-entrepreneurial young adults) or have cared for the poor and needy (41% vs. 22%). Accordingly, they are more likely to look for opportunities to fight injustice when they engage with a church.

Addressing Financial Anxiety

Why is education / career such a dividing line for the emotional stability of adults, especially for today's 18–35-year-olds? Where do you think some of these feelings stem from?

In our society, you need money to do the most basic things like eat, acquire housing or even look for work if you don't have it. People without employment probably feel a lot of anxiety or stress. Even though I have a full-time job, I know how it feels to worry about an upcoming bill. Additionally, our society places a ton of emotional weight on the ability to provide for oneself. We often give it a moral understanding around a person's commitment, devotion and ability. Unemployed people and students have a double bind: They feel the pressures of failure (or potential failure in the case of students) combined with the sadness of not living up to a standard about their commitment and ability imposed on them.

Your church is experimenting in providing debt relief and debt forgiveness as a primary function of its ministry. What are other ways you'd like to see ministries provide practical support to address young adults' concerns about debt and economic anxieties?

Churches have to shift from a standpoint of, "How do we help people struggling with these things?" to "We struggle with these things, so how do we help each other?" Often, people don't want to acknowledge that they struggle with their finances. We need to start talking about such matters. In conversations about debt, I have no problem telling congregants how much I owe in student loans, credit card and other debts.

One practical way churches can help people would be to acknowledge two parts of the problem: A lot of people are in trouble financially, and (this one is key) it's not their fault. More and more Millennials understand that we got a raw deal, generationally. Things cost more and jobs pay less. I would advise church leaders to resist the standard answers to economic and financial problems—financial counseling in particular. A lot of Millennials know that these efforts only reinforce a go-it-alone mentality when we need communal resources and an imagination that allows us to expand our ideas about what we can do together, whether that's paying off each other's debts, organizing a union or taking political power to use our institutions for all people, not just an elite few. ●

JOHN THORNTON JR.
Copastor of Missions & Outreach at
Jubilee Baptist Church (Chapel Hill, NC)
UNITED STATES

Going Abroad

A GLIMPSE OF THE YOUNG ADULTS WHO'VE HAD THE FORMATIVE, FORTUNATE OPPORTUNITY TO TRAVEL INTERNATIONALLY

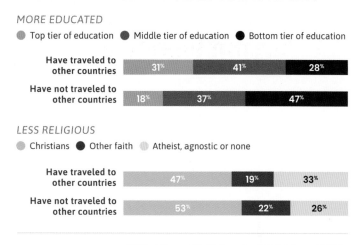

A PROFILE OF WELL-TRAVELED YOUNG ADULTS

MORE EDUCATED

● Top tier of education   ● Middle tier of education   ● Bottom tier of education

Have traveled to other countries: 31% | 41% | 28%

Have not traveled to other countries: 18% | 37% | 47%

LESS RELIGIOUS

● Christians   ● Other faith   ● Atheist, agnostic or none

Have traveled to other countries: 47% | 19% | 33%

Have not traveled to other countries: 53% | 22% | 26%

n=15,369 adults ages 18 to 35, December 4, 2018–February 15, 2019.

One uniquely global narrative to surface in this study: 43 percent of young adults have visited other countries, while one-third (32%) hopes to do so in the next decade.

Though a sense of global connection or even wanderlust is ascribed generally to young adults today, 18–35-year-olds who have actually traveled internationally stand out. Given the means that travel may require, a fairly privileged group comes into focus. Nearly one-third (31%) falls into the top tier of education, and it's possible some journeys have been part of school programs or gap years. Young adults who have gone on trips to other countries often point to multiple other accomplishments such as having achieved financial independence (60% vs. 36% of those who haven't traveled internationally), completed their education (60% vs. 38%), started a career (54% vs. 31%) or purchased a home (29% vs. 14%).

Signs of stability extend to their emotions and relationships too. Compared to their peers who've stuck close to home, they feel more connected to people around the world (62% vs. 53%) and deeply cared for by those around them (40% vs. 28%). More than one-quarter (28%) qualifies as having strong connectivity—though, interestingly, their exposure to other places hasn't significantly increased their concern for others' welfare or engagement in justice work.

From where do young adults embark? Residents of Europe and Oceania are among some of the most likely to travel, while those in Africa report some of the lowest travel rates. Switzerland tops the list (72%); in Ghana, just 9 percent of young adults have visited other nations. An array of factors like affluence, security, access to travel options or proximity to other nations might influence these national trends.

Considering the religious climates of these countries, we see a greater proportion of well-traveled respondents from secular contexts (58% vs. 31% in Christian climates, 43% in multi-faith climates) or with no religious affiliation (33% vs. 26% of those who've never traveled internationally are atheists, agnostics or nones). They have lower opinions of religion's import in society (48% vs. 57% of those who haven't traveled internationally) or their personal life (27% vs. 41%). ◗

The Well-Being Gap

WOMEN LAG BEHIND MEN IN SEVERAL
MARKERS OF EMOTIONAL SECURITY

On the whole, it's reasonable to consider the literate, well-connected 18–35-year-olds in this study as beneficiaries of great global advances in gender justice and equality, with many thanks to the generations preceding them—yet there are still telling discrepancies between the experiences of these young men and young women.

Looking at emotional health, women are more likely than men to report a range of negative feelings, especially anxiety about important decisions (47% vs. 33%) or un-

certainty about the future (45% vs. 34%). Granted, it's possible that women may be more in touch with or at least more open about the troubling emotions they face, while many men around the world still sense cultural pressures that may stifle such introspection or expression. Still, these differences are vexing when reminded of the gaps that *don't* exist between these young men and women today—for instance, overall, they are similarly religious, similarly educated and so on, factors that typically act as boons to well-being.

These disparate emotional experiences appear to be compounded and complicated by whether a man or woman has a job and / or whether a man or woman is raising children. Meaning, in terms of emotional profile alone, women fare worse than men, mothers fare worse than fathers—and mothers who don't work are in a particularly precarious position.

Men are slightly more likely than women to be working, a divide that deepens among parents.

NEGATIVE EMOTIONS AMONG MEN & WOMEN

"I often feel …"

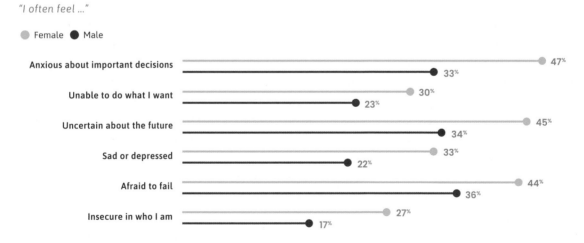

● Female ● Male

	Female	Male
Anxious about important decisions	47%	33%
Unable to do what I want	30%	23%
Uncertain about the future	45%	34%
Sad or depressed	33%	22%
Afraid to fail	44%	36%
Insecure in who I am	27%	17%

n=15,320 adults ages 18 to 35, December 4, 2018–February 15, 2019.

Three in four fathers in this survey (74% vs. 42% of men who are not parents) work full-time, compared to 44 percent of mothers (and 40% of women who are not parents) who report full-time employment. One in four mothers (25%), meanwhile, is a stay-at-home parent, an arrangement that is still rare for fathers (2%).

Though some gender patterns in responses are tempered by employment status, mothers who don't have full-time jobs (a group that represents 46% of all moms in the study) profess the lowest levels of optimism about the future (33%)—lower than working mothers (46%) as well as fathers of any employment status (48% employed, 43% unemployed). Mothers who don't work are more likely than other parenting categories to live in small-town or rural settings (33%), tend to be lonely (27%) and less inclined to sense a connection to the world around them (49%). Accordingly, nearly half of this group of women (46%) score low on Barna's connectivity metric (vs. 30% of working fathers, 35% of unemployed fathers and 32% of working mothers who have weak connectivity). One in three expresses feeling sad or depressed (32%) or unable to do what they want (32%). Thus far into adulthood, they appear to have had a harder time than their working peers when it comes to feeling like they've followed their dreams (21% vs. 36% of working moms) or found out who they really are (33% vs. 40%).

Considering the baseline career-orientation and economic anxiety that pervades this generation (see page 37), combined with recognized barriers to women's professional development and success (which vary significantly in severity across the countries in this study), it's not surprising to see the well-being of women and mothers so tied to the provision, identity or stability that employment suggests. In Barna's previous research in the U.S. alone, we've noted that women's general satisfaction in life and engagement with their vocation wanes as they get married and / or have children, while these positive measures only increase for men as they progress into both career and family.[10] At the same time, we've seen that mothers continue to bear much of the responsibility at home, as support systems for their partners as well as children's primary partners in conversation, recreation and spiritual development.[11]

These dynamics are front of mind for young women in this study of 18–35-year-olds. When asked to think about challenges to leadership, more than one-third of women (35%) identifies gender inequality as one of the world's greatest problems; one in four men (24%) feels the same. Yet, even among Christians alone, men are more likely than women to say they have found support for their professional development in the Church.

For myriad reasons—whether gender discrepancies in pay, domestic labor, parenting expectations or a sense of personal security and safety—the young women in this study show greater vulnerability than their male peers. It's plain that helping 18–35-year-olds navigate career and family are pressing needs of this generation's discipleship and development and, for young women, there may be more twists and turns along the way. ●

Empowering Women

NATASHA SISTRUNK ROBINSON
International speaker, author, executive
leadership coach & consultant,
diversity & mentoring coach
UNITED STATES

REV. DR. LYDIA MWANIKI
Director for Gender, Women and
Youth Department at All Africa
Conference of Churches (AACC)
KENYA

Across this and other studies, the data show men as being more sure of their place in the world compared to women. What do you think contributes to this?

NATASHA: There's equal pressure to feel successful, but men and women aren't giving up the same thing for that success. Women are sacrificing more and getting less, not just in pay, but in life in general. The trajectory of feminism, particularly in the West, has placed an emphasis on making your mark in the world, getting a seat at the table, earning equal pay, busting those glass ceilings. In other words, a lot of the emphasis on feminism has been on life outside the home, and there hasn't been a parallel emphasis among men to invest at home, or to elevate home life. So both genders are elevating work life without a similar emphasis placed on the home. Typically, the people making decisions in the workplace regarding family leave, pay and other aspects of work that affect our lives at home are men. There's a lot of power in that seat at the table in the workplace that directly impacts the home, and I would like to see men have more integrity and intentionality in how they steward that power.

When you're working with and mentoring young women, what are some of the messages you're trying to elevate or lies you're trying to counteract?

NATASHA: Most of the young people I mentor, particularly in my nonprofit, are African-American high school girls, and these are their formative years. I work with a team of men and women of diverse generations, and part of the way we are stewarding, training and influencing them, is by what we model. The way we have healthy male and female relationships. Showing them this is what a healthy marriage looks like. This is what a sisterhood feels like.

I say to the young women who come to us, I don't like giving people pipe dreams. We teach them about basic stuff: You have to work hard. You have to be a person of character. You have to be clear about your purpose. Bad company corrupts good morals. Sometimes they know it's from the Bible, and sometimes they don't, but they're good principles. So we model for them, we talk to them, and then we allow them to practice these various things in their faith, mental health, their health and wellness, because we want to develop them holistically as leaders.

In our leadership summer program, we offer four workshops every year: in media & art, business & entrepreneurship, military & government and STEM (science, technology, engineering and math). We have women leaders expose them to different parts of that career field, and then the girls get active engagement and ask questions. The reason we do that is because those are fields where women are traditionally underrepresented in higher echelons of leadership. A lot of times, women and girls are cut out of the race because they don't even know what's out there and how to prepare.

How does poverty create more vulnerability for women?

LYDIA: Deeply rooted structural obstacles, such as unequal distribution of resources, power and wealth combined with social institutions and norms that sustain inequality, hold African women back. Women and girls are, therefore, often disproportionately affected by poverty because of their already precarious situation due to structurally unequal power relations.

For instance, agriculture is the backbone of most African economies, and smallholder women farmers comprise nearly half of the labor force in Africa's agriculture sector.[12] However, ironically, women remain the majority of the landless. They are increasingly shouldering the burden of family and community care in the African context of war, hunger and disease. The burden of care with little or no resources is an emotional burden to which women are subjected, and unfortunately, it's still connected to discrimination.

There is also gender disparity in valuation of labor, whereby a woman's role is accorded lower status or importance.

What are solutions to begin closing these gender gaps?
LYDIA: At the AACC, we find the following models useful:
- Deconstructing / demolishing hierarchical gender constructions and reconstructing masculinities and femininities in egalitarian ways. Education is a key tool here, engaging all institutions.
- Domesticating and implementing all the legal instruments for gender justice and encouraging religious actors, civil society organizations and non-governmental organizations to hold governments accountable when rights of women are violated. Advocacy about these legal instruments is required among the stakeholders to create awareness about them.
- Promoting women's and youth's entrepreneurial skills development for wealth creation.
- Interpreting and appropriating non-liberating, gendered biblical texts in life-affirming ways. Some texts have been used to reinforce unhelpful cultural beliefs and attitudes toward women not only in the history of the Christian tradition, but in all areas of life.
- Giving legal instruments a biblical and theological basis. This can be done by using biblical and theological models, which offer foundations for gender equality. ●

Connectedness Does Not Equal Community

WHY DO SO FEW YOUNG ADULTS FEEL CARED FOR BY OTHERS?

Our world may be increasingly digitally connected—but the experience of connection in one's daily life isn't a guarantee. *Just one in three 18–35-year-old respondents (33%) says they feel deeply cared for by those around them.* Meanwhile, nearly one in four (23%) encounters feelings of loneliness and isolation.

Looking at the 25 countries included in this study, there are some surprising social trends. The U.S. and Australia top the list in reporting frequent loneliness and isolation (34%), followed by the UK and New Zealand (31% each)—all very Westernized contexts. On the other end of the spectrum, young adults in countries like Indonesia (11%), Kenya (12%), Mexico (13%) and Romania (13%) less often report this kind of detachment.

There are certainly many factors that may shape these social climates, including cultural atittudes that place more value on either individualism or community, either career or personal life and so on. It's worth noting too that many of the **nations regarded as developed or affluent show noticeably higher degrees of reported loneliness.**[13] For example, Mexico and Romania, are among both the least affluent surveyed countries and the least likely to be associated with loneliness. Meanwhile, many countries where respondents report being isolated are more affluent than their continental neighbors, as in the case of Chile (28% vs. 16% in Colombia and Brazil) and South Africa (26% vs. 12% in Kenya, 15% in Nigeria, and 16% in Ghana). Despite having access and resources that might foster connectivity on a broader scale, respondents in most of the countries where loneliness is prevalent also tend to feel less connected to people around the world, indicating a consistent lack of relational richness.

When it comes to countering loneliness on a personal level, respondents who belong to a faith tradition seem to have stronger feelings of being in relationship with others. Respondents who identify with Christianity (19%) or other faiths (22%) are less inclined than their counterparts without a faith (31%) to say they feel isolated. This effect is emphasized when sorting religious respondents by

JUST ONE IN THREE YOUNG ADULTS SAYS THEY FEEL DEEPLY CARED FOR BY THOSE AROUND THEM

those who value and are active in their faith (16% of practicing Christians, 15% of practicing adherents of another faith vs. 21% of non-practicing Christians, 25% of non-practicing adherents of another faith). This apparent relationship between faith and a sense of belonging is not definitive, and it should be considered that some of these religious respondents are not as willing to recognize or express negative emotions such as isolation. However, we do see evidence that some key mentorships and friendships are common among young Christians, and patterns in the data at least suggest *religion may play some role in keeping loneliness at bay.* ●

WHERE DO YOUNG ADULTS FEEL LONELY & ISOLATED?

Countries divided by religious climate

● Christian climate ● Multi-faith climate ● Secular climate

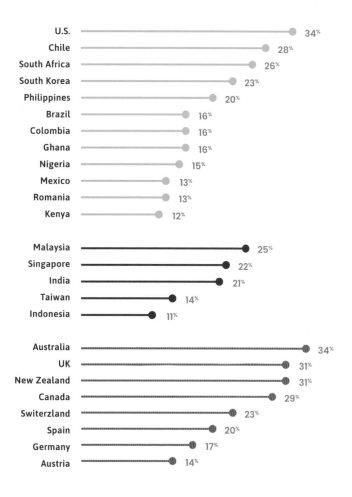

U.S.	34%
Chile	28%
South Africa	26%
South Korea	23%
Philippines	20%
Brazil	16%
Colombia	16%
Ghana	16%
Nigeria	15%
Mexico	13%
Romania	13%
Kenya	12%
Malaysia	25%
Singapore	22%
India	21%
Taiwan	14%
Indonesia	11%
Australia	34%
UK	31%
New Zealand	31%
Canada	29%
Switerzland	23%
Spain	20%
Germany	17%
Austria	14%

n=15,369 adults ages 18 to 35, December 4, 2018–February 15, 2019.

THE EMOTIONAL CLIMATE OF A CONNECTED GENERATION

MIXED EMOTIONS ABOUT MOVING FORWARD

The 18–35-year-olds in this survey are just as likely to feel optimistic as uncertain about the future (40% each). In fact, 28 percent feel both optimistic and uncertain as they look ahead. There are a number of life factors that may influence a young adult's feelings about the future, including faith practice, employment and relationship status.

"I OFTEN FEEL ..."

● Positive emotions ● Negative emotions

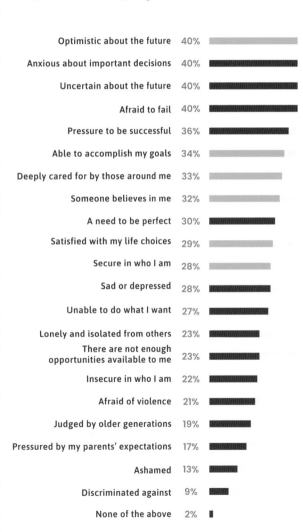

Optimistic about the future	40%
Anxious about important decisions	40%
Uncertain about the future	40%
Afraid to fail	40%
Pressure to be successful	36%
Able to accomplish my goals	34%
Deeply cared for by those around me	33%
Someone believes in me	32%
A need to be perfect	30%
Satisfied with my life choices	29%
Secure in who I am	28%
Sad or depressed	28%
Unable to do what I want	27%
Lonely and isolated from others	23%
There are not enough opportunities available to me	23%
Insecure in who I am	22%
Afraid of violence	21%
Judged by older generations	19%
Pressured by my parents' expectations	17%
Ashamed	13%
Discriminated against	9%
None of the above	2%

● No faith
● Non-practicing other faith
● Practicing other faith
● Non-practicing Christian
● Practicing Christian

● All working
● Self-employed
● Students
● All unemployed
● Married
● All single

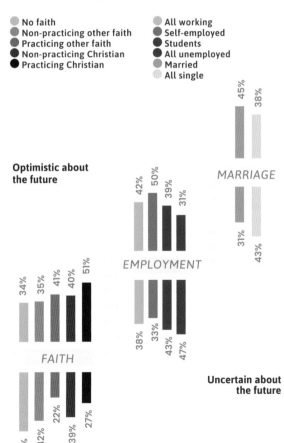

n≈15,369 adults ages 18 to 35, December 4, 2018–February 15, 2019.

Representatives of an Age of Anxiety

WORRISOME TRUTHS ABOUT THE MENTAL AND
EMOTIONAL WELL-BEING OF 18–35-YEAR-OLDS TODAY

Throughout this study, there are several signs that 18–35-year-olds are not quite at ease in the world— a main one being that they tell us so. ***Respondents had an opportunity to provide a portrait of their emotions, and the image is one of a generation gripped by worry.*** Anxiety about important decisions is widespread (40%), as well as uncertainty about the future (40%), a fear of failure (40%) and a pressure to be successful (36%). Though this study alone can't speak to actual diagnoses of mental illness, nearly three in 10 overall (28%) call themselves sad or depressed.

Some of these negative emotions are fairly common across the sample—general worry about big decisions, for instance, is not so exclusive to particular segments or contexts. To recognize the prevalence or severity of deep anxiety among this connected generation, Barna grouped respondents into an "anxious" category if they say they feel at least three of the following: anxious about important decisions, sad or depressed, afraid of failure and / or insecure in who they are. Overall, one in five young adults (20%) meets this more pointed qualification. They're also a group that is more likely to experience other negative emotions included in the survey, from a lack of opportunity to a sense of being judged by older generations.

This is a select group of young adults who, in addition to ranking low in connectivity (45%), are clearly under significant strain. How can church leaders support their well-being? To summarize this section of the report and our findings about this generation thus far: Addressing the anxious state of 18–35-year-olds today also means addressing vocation, money, community and spiritual growth.

The Stress of Striving

Financial and professional instability may contribute to the spread of this anxiety epidemic. A global survey from Deloitte highlights the pervasive pessimism Millennials feel about the economy at large and their personal employment.[14] A study from the American Psychiatric Association found that, across several factors that might influence mental well-being— such as health, safety, finances, relationships and politics—Millennials most often felt anxious about paying bills.[15] Research out of England and Wales shows that worries about money and cost of housing (in addition to concern over Brexit) are driving a recent surge in anxiety of young women.[16] In a viral BuzzFeed article, journalist Anne Helen Peterson reflects on how her U.S. Millennial peers have become, as she calls them, "the burnout generation"—and she primarily points the finger at unrealistic expectations for academic, professional and financial success. "Efficiency was supposed to give us more job security, more pay, perhaps even more leisure," she writes. "Our efficiency hasn't bucked wage stagnation; our steadfastness hasn't made us more valuable."[17]

In this Barna study, when controlling for several factors at both local and global levels, financial security is among the greatest predictors of anxiety. Relatedly, anxiety fades somewhat among respondents with more stable employment (18% working vs. 27% unemployed show markers of anxiety) and among those on the older end of the 18 to 35 age range. Thus, as they look toward the next decade of life, those who express emotional or mental insecurity are especially concerned about starting their career (44%) and gaining financial independence (43%)—goals that have, so far, shaped the aims and identity of the connected generation (see page 37).

The Anxious Feel Like They're on Their Own

The majority of respondents under great stress also says they are lonely. *An alarming six in 10 in the group that expresses a series of anxious feelings (59%)—compared to one-quarter of all respondents—reports a sense of isolation.*

When segmented by their marital status, we see one relational dimension to anxiety. Generally, respondents who have spouses have lower odds of experiencing such fears and insecurities (12% married vs. 23% single qualify as anxious).

Anxious young adults, perhaps sensing their detachment, are more likely to cite relational motivations for participating in communities of worship, such as being involved in community (34% vs. 23% overall) or accompanying family members (29% vs 20%). Thinking about what's missing from their place of worship, friends (23%) and support groups (19%) are top of mind.

Faith communities may be seen as facilitators of connection for troubled 18–35-year-olds—but getting them in the door may be a challenge. Roughly one in five respondents who experience levels of anxiety (22%) attends a place of worship weekly, compared to one-third of others (33% of those who don't qualify as anxious). Instead, these more anxious adults are twice as likely as others to say they used to attend a place of worship, suggesting a move away from faith engagement over time. This may be because they are on the fence, at best, when it comes to the perceived value of spirituality and religion. Respondents with heightened worries experience heightened doubts; they are more likely than others to note that issues like hypocrisy (43% vs. 29%), human suffering (41% vs. 25%), global conflict (38% vs. 24%) or unanswered prayer (27% vs. 13%) are barriers to their belief in a spiritual dimension. They are less likely to express that religion is good for people (48% vs. 57% overall) or society (43% vs. 53%) and similarly hesitant to embrace the influence of the Christian Church (39% vs. 47% say it's important to society).

On a personal level, only about one-third of anxious respondents agrees faith plays a central role in their own life (35% vs. 44% of those who don't qualify as anxious). Looking at affiliation, many of the negative feelings listed in this survey, including those that may be associated with anxiety, are more common among those who don't identify with faith—28 percent of atheists, agnostics and "nones" report this level of unrest, significantly more than the percentage of Christians (16%) and other religious respondents (17%) who do.

Which comes first, lack of faith or anxiety? Disconnection or anxiety? Do anxieties blossom in the absence of community or belief—or have people found religion and relationships are ill-equipped to address their existing worries? This study can't speak to the direction of these correlations, and they may be cyclical. What we know, from our own research and others, is there is no shortage of factors that may amplify a generational tendency toward anxiety: Internet activity that adds to overwhelming worries and robs rest from 18–35-year-olds today.[18] The fear of the unknown, the pressure to succeed and the weight of comparisons to others during college years, financially lean years or single years. A lack of strong roots in religious practice, which can be beneficial to one's spiritual, relational and mental health.[19]

It's also important to consider, however, that this heightened awareness of and willingness to acknowledge anxiety may be a sign of improvement, a product of years spent chipping away at taboos surrounding mental health. Conversations about stress, fear and burnout among the connected generation could represent not just crisis, but openness. Either way, it represents an opportunity for the Church—to directly address anxiety, as well as the spiritual, digital, relational and financial circumstances that nurture it. ●

SIGNS OF ANXIETY

"I often feel …"

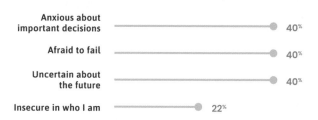

Anxious about important decisions	40%
Afraid to fail	40%
Uncertain about the future	40%
Insecure in who I am	22%

Feel at least three of these emotions

● Total ● Christians ● Other faith ● No faith

20%   16%   17%   28%

n=15,369 adults ages 18 to 35, December 4, 2018–February 15, 2019.

COUNTRY COMPARISON

SIGNS
OF ANXIETY

On average, one in five 18–35-year-olds around the globe identifies with feelings related to anxiety—specifically, they report feeling at least three of the four following emotions: anxiety about important decisions, sadness or depression, fear of failure and insecurity in themselves. There are some continental, and perhaps cultural, trends in this regard, though not in the way one might assume; some of the nations with the most means or opportunity are also among the most likely to present (or, perhaps, to acknowledge) feelings of anxiety. For example, those in North America and Oceania are more likely to fall into this segment, while respondents in African countries are less likely to report these apprehensions.

Country	%
AUSTRALIA	28%
AUSTRIA	9%
BRAZIL	16%
CANADA	27%
CHILE	20%
COLOMBIA	10%
GERMANY	14%
GHANA	9%
INDIA	10%
INDONESIA	10%
KENYA	11%
MALAYSIA	18%
MEXICO	9%
NEW ZEALAND	29%
NIGERIA	12%
PHILIPPINES	20%
ROMANIA	14%
SINGAPORE	18%
SOUTH AFRICA	22%
SOUTH KOREA	22%
SPAIN	14%
SWITZERLAND	16%
TAIWAN	32%
UNITED KINGDOM	27%
UNITED STATES	29%

n=15,369 adults ages 18 to 35, December 4, 2018–February 15, 2019.

Q & A

Harnessing a Global Awareness

How has being globally minded affected this generation's behaviors?

Perhaps the most fundamental impact are changes in the way they relate or commit. Relationships seem more fragile, commitment more taxing. Committing to a specific something—friend or cause, neighborhood or partner, faith community or global concern—is a real discipleship challenge.

How can churches engage this global awareness as they disciple 18–35-year-olds, particularly in secular climates?

First, help Millennials experience a global need personally, deeply and relationally. We encourage them to live in an intentional mission community in Kolkata for short periods of time and sense where God is at work there. Our prayer is for each person to meet God in the lives of one of the poor they meet—someone whose life they cannot forget and whose realities will shape their life choices. Second, we encourage them to make time-framed commitments to mission tasks (e.g. being a youth leader or prison visitor) or living in a locally based community for a few years. Choosing this commitment means saying no to other relationships and opportunities, but it also means experiencing the depth of friendship or service in ways that link us to God and each other in personally transformative, rich and life-shaping ways.

Can you share about how your church responded after the Christchurch mosque shootings in 2019?

As a relatively large church of around 2,000 attenders and 19 entities working in the community, we collectively employ over 400 people in mental health, youth, community development, prison support, pre-schools and social housing. We are heavily involved in the government's pilot community-based sponsorship of refugees programme. Our church has direct friendships to many of the families in which people were injured or killed in March 2019. The impact was four-fold. First, and ongoing, was the immediate need to care for the bereaved and injured. Second, we sought to care for those indirectly involved, (police, medical staff, teachers). Thirdly, churches and organizations looked to us as an example and key provider, which led to conversations and direct support of affected families. Lastly, the government approached us to help establish a second pilot project to bring refugees into New Zealand through a new community-based sponsorship scheme. ●

ALAN JAMIESON
Senior Pastor, South West Baptist Church (Christchurch)
NEW ZEALAND

Q & A

Building Toward the Future

How do you see higher levels of loneliness and anxiety playing out in the lives of young people?

Our generation has a huge amount of difficulty because we're trying to get meaning and purpose and health—all these things that everyone's always wanted—but we're being forced to get those from a smaller select group of things. Realistically, the promise the world is giving us, in a consumeristic mentality, is an individualistic dream or promise.

The meaning or connection you get from neighborhood, from family, from living in one location your whole life, from religion … all these things that really anchor you are starting to go away, one by one. Because we think, as a culture, those are harmful; they seem to limit us, and limits are considered evil in our culture. I think that leads us to disillusionment, which then becomes anxiety: "Oh, this is not what I'm created for. There's got to be more." There's tension. There's wrestling. You see everyone else seeming like they're doing OK.

How can spiritual growth come out of the frantic nature and pressures of this culture?

I'd love to see people return to more of a hyper-relational discipleship. Bringing people into and joining rhythms—that's where there's a lot more of the richness or relationship of actual discipleship. When you look at Jesus' life, that's how it happens. Life on life. Walking with one another.

There's a level to which we learn and are taught better when we are next to someone going about their life. We need to get back to that, but that's really antithetical to our moment. Because that's very invasive, and we don't like our space be-

ing invaded. It's very vulnerable, it's very uncontrollable. All those things are really difficult for us right now, but I think that's where actual discipleship happens.

What message do you think older generations need to hear about your generation?

I believe the older generation has something to say. Youth is the ideal in our culture; a 25-year-old Silicon Valley tech person is basically the ideal of what we should pursue today, but in the scriptures, it says if you have gray hair, that's the ideal. We have competing pictures of what the finish line should be. Because of that, I think old people are being moved aside. But it's clear in scripture that you actually should build toward old age, and then old age is like this afterglow season, when you can unleash the wisdom God has formed in you for the development of resilient disciples. ●

JEFFERSON BETHKE
Author, speaker, podcaster
UNITED STATES

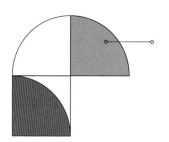

Connect the Dots:
Life in an Anxious Age

REFLECTIONS AND NEXT STEPS
INSPIRED BY THE RESEARCH

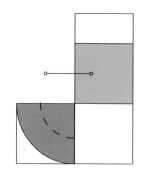

See the whole.

- Paradoxes and contradictions are at the heart of the connected generation. For instance, they are more globally linked than previous generations, and yet they are often lonely and isolated from their surrounding community.
- Global connectedness brings both opportunities and challenges. Many young adults feel uncertainty related to vocation and economics (especially students) and anxiety about their shared future.
- The experiences of Millennial and Gen Z women are often quite different from the young men who are their generational peers. Young mothers, in particular, don't seem to feel the benefits of connectivity as much as other groups.

Take time to pray.

- For Millennials and Gen Z teens who feel isolated and relationally disconnected; for those who feel uncertain, insecure or anxious; for young women (especially mothers) who are more likely to experience these feelings.

- For young people in your cultural context, with its unique pressures and challenges; for vocational and educational opportunities; for comfort for the lonely and encouragement for the fearful.
- For your community to respond with grace, wisdom and understanding to the needs of teens and young adults in various stages of life; for opportunities to bring care and connectivity where there is chaos.

Create what's next.

- *Listen.* Each young person has a story—and most want to tell it! Learning starts with listening. The same goes for relationships.
- *Think.* How are you helping people get and stay connected to each other and to God? How is it going? Should you do less, more, the same or different?
- *Act.* Model and espouse a balanced use of digital tools that leads to better, deeper and fruitful connectivity.

ENGAGEMENT WITH

NEARLY THREE-QUARTERS of young practicing Christians say there is someone in their life who encourages them to grow spiritually.

ALMOST HALF of young adults who have left Christianity see it as "hypocritical," compared to three in 10 of those who've never been Christians.

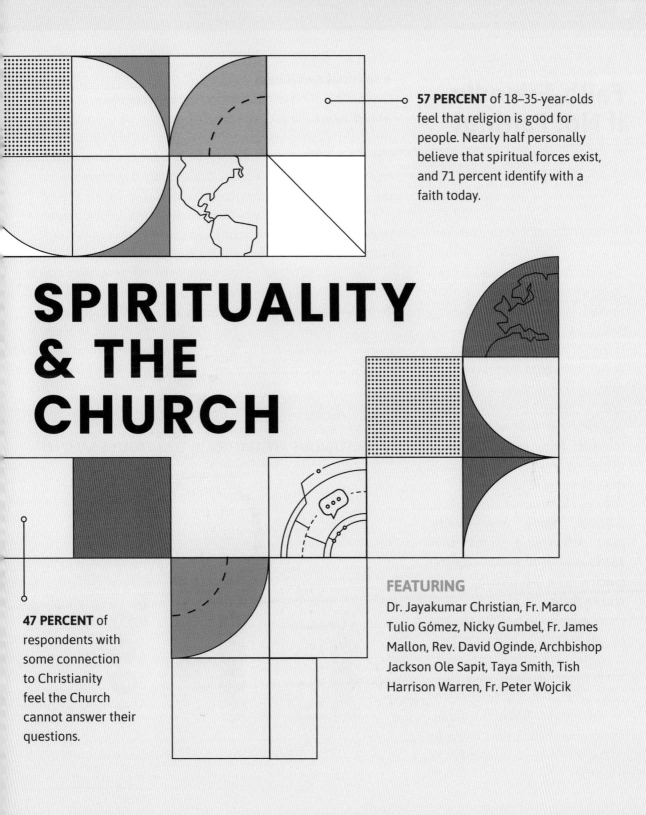

57 PERCENT of 18–35-year-olds feel that religion is good for people. Nearly half personally believe that spiritual forces exist, and 71 percent identify with a faith today.

SPIRITUALITY & THE CHURCH

47 PERCENT of respondents with some connection to Christianity feel the Church cannot answer their questions.

FEATURING

Dr. Jayakumar Christian, Fr. Marco Tulio Gómez, Nicky Gumbel, Fr. James Mallon, Rev. David Oginde, Archbishop Jackson Ole Sapit, Taya Smith, Tish Harrison Warren, Fr. Peter Wojcik

Faith-Friendly, if Not Faithful

MOST 18–35-YEAR-OLDS SEE
THE BENEFITS OF BELIEF

Several nations included in this study are secularized or now witnessing a decline in religion's influence, something Barna has recorded in detail in previous research specific to the U.S. and Europe. In this study, just over one-fifth of 18–35-year-olds (22%) was raised outside of a religious tradition. Three in 10 (29%) identify as atheist, agnostic or simply irreligious today.

When looking at the whole, however, ***there are steady, even surprising signs that 18–35-year-olds remain appreciative of or personally receptive to faith***. We glean this from some willingness to affiliate—half of this sample (51%) are Christians of some stripe, and one in five (20%) belongs to Islam (8%), Hinduism (4%) Buddhism (4%) or other faiths—but also from favorable, and widely held, opinions of the concepts of spirituality or religion.

A Spiritual Awareness

Overall, 18–35-year-olds around the world express an overwhelming openness to spirituality—or, at least, the possibility of a spiritual dimension. Three-quarters are either certain spiritual forces exist (47%) or admit they think they may exist, even if they are unsure (28%). Only 8 percent reject the idea altogether. Though certainty wanes among young adults who identify as atheist, agnostic or irreligious, nearly half are open to the possibility of a spiritual realm (18% are certain spiritual forces exist, 29% think they might).

These numbers are, predictably, even higher among the one in four respondents who practices a religion (by Barna's definition, practicing faith extends beyond affiliation alone to an expressed personal value of one's faith and at least monthly attendance in a community of worship). An embrace of the spiritual is naturally commonplace for practic-

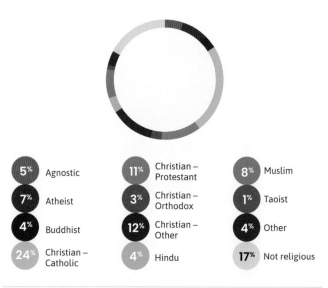

RELIGIOUS AFFILIATION IN THIS STUDY'S SAMPLE

5% Agnostic	11% Christian – Protestant	8% Muslim
7% Atheist	3% Christian – Orthodox	1% Taoist
4% Buddhist	12% Christian – Other	4% Other
24% Christian – Catholic	4% Hindu	17% Not religious

n=15,369 adults ages 18 to 35, December 4, 2018–February 15, 2019.
Some religions included in the questionnaire are not shown here as they were selected by less than 1 percent. This includes respondents who identify with Judaism, Sikhism or Confucianism.

ing Christians as well as those who practice other faiths (94% and 89%, respectively, are certain or think spiritual forces exist), compared to those who are atheist, agnostic or unaffiliated (47%). There is an interesting divergence with non-practicing religious respondents—that is, those who identify with a faith but do not see it as very personally important or do not regularly attend a worship community. While four of five practicing Christians (81%) express complete certainty that spiritual forces exist, slightly less than half of non-practicing Christians (45%) share their confidence. This trend is also present among practicing and non-practicing members of other religious traditions (73% vs. 47%).

Naturally, this correlation between belief in the spiritual and personal religious practice can be seen collectively across religious climates. More than four in five respondents from more religious cultures express openness to believing in spiritual forces (83% Christian, 87% multifaith), but nearly two-thirds living in what Barna describes as post-Christian or secular environments (62%) share the same openness.

However, there are some barriers to belief in a spiritual dimension—a top one being spiritually engaged people themselves. One in three young adults (32%) says that hypocrisy of religious people causes them to doubt things of a spiritual dimension. Science also challenges respondents' willingness to believe (31%). In keeping with the generations' global awareness and inclinations toward justice, ***more than a quarter of 18–35-year-olds points to human suffering (28%) or conflict around the world (26%) as reasons they might have doubts***. All of these factors prove to be bigger obstacles among people who don't identify with a religion (46% science, 43% hypocrisy of religious people, 35% human suffering, 32% conflict in the world). Though this ranking of reasons to doubt follows a similar pattern among religious respondents, the plurality of practicing members of Christianity (40%) and other faiths (31%) says nothing makes them question the reality of spirituality.

General Warmth Toward Religion

While this generation concedes the existence of spiritual forces—a slippery term that can have a variety of definitions—does this mean they are similarly open to organized, religious understandings of spirituality?

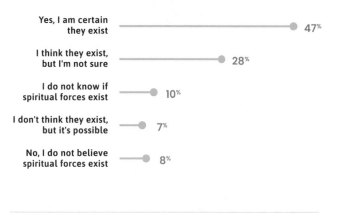

DO YOU BELIEVE IN SPIRITUAL FORCES?

Yes, I am certain they exist — 47%
I think they exist, but I'm not sure — 28%
I do not know if spiritual forces exist — 10%
I don't think they exist, but it's possible — 7%
No, I do not believe spiritual forces exist — 8%

n=15,369 adults ages 18 to 35, December 4, 2018–February 15, 2019.

IDEAS ABOUT THE ROLE OF RELIGION

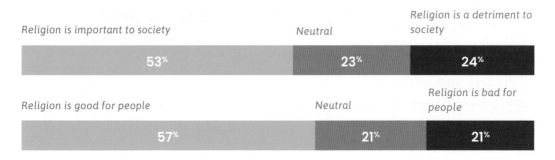

Religion is important to society   Neutral   Religion is a detriment to society

| 53% | 23% | 24% |

Religion is good for people   Neutral   Religion is bad for people

| 57% | 21% | 21% |

n=15,369 adults ages 18 to 35, December 4, 2018–February 15, 2019.

Overall, ***more than half of the 18–35-year-olds polled (57%) feel that religion is good for people***; one in five holds a neutral opinion or asserts religion is bad for people (21% each). Young adults give similar responses when asked about religion's value to society in general, with more than half (53%) saying it is important, rather than a detriment (24%).

Those who engage meaningfully with their faith espouse the benefits of religion, both for individuals (89% among practicing Christians and 84% among those practicing other faiths) and society (86% and 81%). Non-practicing members of faith traditions fall more in line with the average in their warmth toward religion. Unsurprisingly, more opposition appears among those who do not identify with a faith: Around half of these respondents view religion as bad for people (48%) or a detriment to society (51%). Still, ***even among the irreligious, one-fifth regards religion as a positive thing for individuals (21%) or societies (18%).***

Here, too, we see a pattern across different faith climates. In more religious contexts, two-thirds of respondents welcome religion as a good thing for people (66% Christian, 65% multi-faith) and crucial for society (63% and 61%). In secular contexts, less than half feel the same way (45% say it's good for people, 40% say it's important to society), with one-third expressing concern about religion's impact instead (30% say it's bad for people, 33% say it's a detriment to society).

Acting on Spiritual Interest

Do these mostly positive views about spirituality and religion at large seep into the identities or daily actions of young adults? About three in five respondents agree at least in part with the statement "My religious faith is very important to my life today" (35% strongly agree + 26% somewhat agree). These numbers are slightly higher in countries with strong religious climates (73% Christian, 72% multi-faith) and markedly lower in secular climates (42%).

Half of all 18–35-year-olds in the study (51%) say they participate in private prayer at least monthly. These percentages climb for respondents who also call themselves religious (72% Christians, 56% other faiths), but even among those of no faith, 13 percent report praying on their own at this frequency. (Among Christians, particularly practicing Christians, there are boosts in engagement in prayer and a number of other spiritual disciplines, as explored on page 74.)

While these responses suggest a dynamic spiritual disposition in this generation, percentages for regular attendance of religious services aren't particularly notable. Of those who are part of a faith group, slightly more than half say that they attend religious services on a monthly basis (31% once a week + 14% a few times a month + 7% once a month). Another quarter of those who are part of a faith group says they attend at least once a year (12% a few times every six months + 12% once or twice

Media for Spiritual Growth

How does an often device-dependent, hyper-connected generation invest time in learning about faith? Barna presented respondents with several media-driven tools for spiritual growth, asking if 18–35-year-olds use these faith-based resources on a monthly basis:

- worship music (29%)
- books (28%)
- videos or TV (23%)
- podcasts and radio broadcasts (22%)
- social media (22%)
- none (48%)

Naturally, those who don't claim faith are highly unlikely to pursue any of this content (86% "none of these"). All religious respondents favor these options similarly, with the exception of worship music, which Christians are much more likely to listen to (46%, compared to 22% of people of other faiths). Still, about one-third of members of Christianity (32%) and other religions (35%) doesn't use any of these media to learn from religious speakers and leaders.

a year). Those who qualify as practicing religious respondents, however, exhibit great consistency: Seven in 10 in these segments attend a religious service on a weekly basis (71% practicing Christians, 69% practicing other faiths).

All things considered, 18–35-year-olds around the globe—though occasionally concerned about or even hostile toward religion—appear to lean into the spiritual dimensions of their lives. And, for a devout minority, these predilections turn into vibrant, rewarding disciplines. ●

COUNTRY COMPARISON

SPIRITUAL OPENNESS

"Do you believe in spiritual forces or things of a spiritual dimension?"

● Yes, I'm certain   ● I think so, but I'm not sure   ● I don't know   ● I don't think so, but it's possible   ● No

AUSTRALIA
- 35%
- 30%
- 13%
- 9%
- 11%

AUSTRIA
- 28%
- 29%
- 16%
- 13%
- 14%

BRAZIL
- 64%
- 22%
- 5%
- 4%
- 4%

CANADA
- 41%
- 28%
- 12%
- 9%
- 10%

CHILE
- 50%
- 31%
- 3%
- 7%
- 8%

COLOMBIA
- 58%
- 26%
- 7%
- 4%
- 6%

GERMANY
- 25%
- 27%
- 17%
- 11%
- 20%

GHANA
- 81%
- 14%
- 1%
- 1%
- 2%

INDIA
- 44%
- 37%
- 7%
- 5%
- 7%

INDONESIA
- 75%
- 16%
- 4%
- 3%
- 1%

KENYA
- 72%
- 18%
- 2%
- 3%
- 4%

MALAYSIA
- 64%
- 27%
- 4%
- 2%
- 3%

MEXICO
- 50%
- 33%
- 6%
- 6%
- 4%

NEW ZEALAND
- 35%
- 32%
- 13%
- 9%
- 11%

NIGERIA
- 73%
- 18%
- 3%
- 4%
- 2%

PHILIPPINES
- 59%
- 32%
- 4%
- 3%
- 2%

ROMANIA
- 48%
- 28%
- 10%
- 8%
- 6%

SINGAPORE
- 43%
- 39%
- 9%
- 6%
- 3%

SOUTH AFRICA
- 62%
- 24%
- 5%
- 5%
- 4%

SOUTH KOREA
- 21%
- 36%
- 15%
- 14%
- 15%

SPAIN
- 28%
- 28%
- 12%
- 9%
- 13%

SWITZERLAND
- 30%
- 24%
- 16%
- 14%
- 16%

TAIWAN
- 48%
- 42%
- 7%
- 2%
- 0%

UNITED KINGDOM
- 31%
- 30%
- 15%
- 11%
- 12%

UNITED STATES
- 49%
- 28%
- 9%
- 6%
- 7%

n=15,369 adults ages 18 to 35, December 4, 2018–February 15, 2019.

How Religious Context Relates to Religious Practice

A SNAPSHOT OF AFFILIATION, ATTENDANCE AND GENEROSITY ACROSS CHRISTIAN, MULTI-FAITH AND SECULAR CLIMATES

In learning about the faith of 18–35-year-olds in 25 countries around the world, Barna wanted to focus not only on personal faith but on faith environments. By looking at religious climates or cultures, we gauge spiritual norms and dispositions for young adults in various contexts.

It's clear that, in environments where religion is culturally impactful, it is also seen as personally important. (See page 14 for a breakdown of how Barna determined this study's three religious climates and how the locations included in this study are categorized.) In countries where religion has broad societal influence, 18–35-year-olds are more likely to strongly agree that faith is very important in their life—both in Christian contexts (48%) and in multi-faith contexts (44%) On several measures, we see this expressed value of religion carried out.

Religious Affiliation

Across the religious climates, there are predictable patterns in religious affiliation in young adults' present lives as well as their growing-up years. *Those who live in non-Christian or multi-faith contexts are most likely to say they have always been religious* (84%), followed by Christian cultures (69%) and then secular climates (51%). In the last, there is a greater chance of always having

been irreligious (28% vs. 12% Christian climates, 8% multi-faith climates) or of having left the religion of one's youth (14% vs. 11% Christian climates, 4% multi-faith climates). Similarly, if an 18–35-year-old grew up identifying with a religion, there's a greater chance they were at least somewhat active in that faith as a teen (73% Christian climates, 69% multi-faith climates, 56% secular climates were "very" + "somewhat" active).

Affiliation in secular climates is rather low; 41 percent of respondents in these regions identify as atheist, agnostic or with no faith. In Christian climates, Christianity naturally leads as the majority religion, with two of three young adults in these contexts (65%) claiming the faith. Meanwhile, three-quarters of those in other or multi-religious environments are affiliated, usually with major world religions like Islam (34%), Hinduism (20%) or Buddhism (16%).

Religious Services

Attendance of religious services (other than weddings or funerals) is under-

ACROSS CONTEXTS, THERE IS A SOMEWHAT PERVASIVE SENSE THAT ATTENDING A PLACE OF WORSHIP IS A MEANS OF LIVING OUT ONE'S FAITH

standably higher in areas where a religion still has significant cultural influence. In Christian contexts (41%) or in cultures characterized by other faiths (32%), the plurality of young adults who belong to a faith group attends a service once a week or more (compared to 15% of those in countries with predominantly secular societies). More than seven in 10 religious respondents in climates shaped by Christianity (73%) or other faiths (71%) attend at least a few times every six months; less than half of religious respondents in secular contexts (44%) report attending a religious service with this kind of frequency, with as many as one-quarter (26%) saying they never attend.

What brings these 18–35-year-olds with a record of regular attendance into their place of worship? Regardless of their religious climate, most indicate a desire to deepen their spiritual knowledge, a reason that is especially popular in nations that are or were influenced by Christianity. Growing in faith (65% Christian climates, 50% secular climates, 46% multi-faith climates) or learning about God (63% Christian climates, 47% secular climates, 37% multi-faith climates) top the list of motivations. Practicing respondents in Christian cultures continue to emphasize this theme, being more likely to express a desire for wisdom and relevant teachings. (See page 92 for more about why Christians participate in their worship community.) Across contexts, there is a somewhat pervasive sense that attending a place of worship is a means of living out one's faith (39% Christian climates, 36% secular climates, 28% multi-faith climates) or that it is simply the right thing to do (34% Christian climates, 28% secular climates, 30% multi-faith climates).

Religious Expression

Those in Christian contexts lead across a range of other spiritual practices, including personal and group prayer (65% and 41%, respectively), reading scripture (36%), telling others about their beliefs (30%) and attending small groups (17%)—disciplines that are particularly central to the Christian faith.

A general sense of faith-motivated generosity, however, is important to respondents in all religious areas. *Those in cultures shaped by Chris-*

ROLE OF FAITH THROUGHOUT LIFE, ACROSS RELIGIOUS CLIMATES

● Christian climate ● Multi-faith climate ● Secular climate

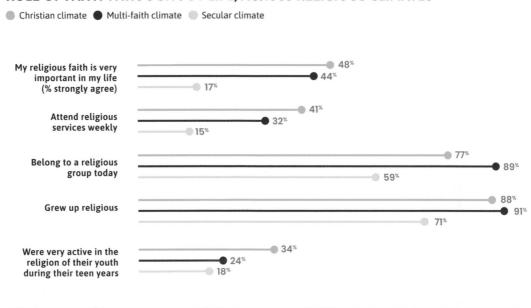

My religious faith is very important in my life (% strongly agree)
48%
44%
17%

Attend religious services weekly
41%
32%
15%

Belong to a religious group today
77%
89%
59%

Grew up religious
88%
91%
71%

Were very active in the religion of their youth during their teen years
34%
24%
18%

n=15,369 adults ages 18 to 35, December 4, 2018–February 15, 2019.

tianity or other religions are more likely than those in secular contexts to volunteer their time (25% Christian climates, 25% multi-faith climates, 17% secular climates) or give to a place of worship (25% Christian climates, 22% multi-faith climates, 10% secular climates), and those in multi-faith climates are especially inclined to give to local charities (26% vs. 17% Christian climates, 15% secular climates). This could be because those in religious contexts are likely to say their belief system motivates them to give of their time (56% Christian climates, 56% multi-faith climates,

37% secular climates) or their resources (48% Christian climates, 48% multi-faith climates, 30% secular climates) to help others in need. In Christian climates, 18–35-year-olds are particularly inclined to feel concern for others' welfare (56% vs. 44% multi-faith climates, 44% secular climates) or take a stand against injustice (51% vs. 41% multi-faith climates, 40% secular climates) or corruption (54% vs. 43% multi-faith climates, 33% secular climates). ●

Q & A

Ministry Across Religious Climates

IN A SECULAR CONTEXT

NICKY GUMBEL
Pioneer of Alpha, vicar of Holy
Trinity Brompton Church in London
UNITED KINGDOM

What have you learned about young adults as you've interacted closely and on a deep level with them over the past 30 years?
I've led 87 Alpha small groups for 18–35-year-olds over the past 30 years. With every course I lead, there are trends that surface. Atheism was big five or six years ago. Now, it's kind of died. In the past, prayers sounded really boring. Now, everybody prays because it's like mindfulness. Healing used to be a difficult concept to teach on. Today, there's so much out there in the secular world about

healing, and people think, why not? Culture is always shifting and evolving.

Do you see opportunities for the gospel that are unique to this generation?
There have been times in history when people have asked, *How can I know God? How can I be saved?* I think the big question people are asking now is, *How can I find meaning—purpose—in life?* That is a huge opportunity. What are we living for? Every human being is asking that question. That is the question to which the gospel is the answer for this generation.

People are also asking, *Where do you find community? Where do you find a marriage partner?* Unless you work in an organization where there are masses of people, which most people don't, there's a pretty limited number of people you can know. Church is one of the very few places anywhere where people find real community, and the only place where you're going to find unconditional love and acceptance.

Human suffering is a big obstacle for people in embracing the Christian faith. What can the Church do to respond to related questions?
On the first night of Alpha, we always ask, *If it turned out there was a God after all, and you could ask one question, what would it be?* It's always the question of why God allows suffering; this is the biggest objection to Christianity. And there is no easy answer to it. The internet has changed the world because knowledge is available to everybody. You can't not be exposed to the suffering of the world. Ultimately, the only an-

swer to it is in Jesus, who suffered for us and suffers with us. So that is the answer, but it's much harder to get to. We've got to answer their questions, but more importantly,

they want to know what we're doing about [suffering]. If the Church is doing nothing and is not engaged in social action against homelessness, poverty, racial injustice, climate change or any of these issues, young people are not going to be very interested.

IN A CHRISTIAN CONTEXT

JACKSON OLE SAPIT
Archbishop of the Anglican
Church of Kenya
KENYA

What is the religious landscape in Kenya right now, and how does Christianity fit into it?

Kenya is a deeply religious country because nearly all Africans and every tribe has a faith in a god of some kind. Today, Kenya is about 80 percent Christian, 10 percent Muslim, and the rest are considered traditionalists.[20] Since 1844, when the modern missionary movement began in our country, Kenya has embraced Christianity. It wasn't hard for Christianity to penetrate into the landscape of Kenya because these are people who already have a belief in a god. There is a big disconnect, however, between Christian faith and Christian practice. Many of us profess to be Christians, but it's increasingly difficult to see how it's impacted our everyday life.

The youths, which make up about the majority of Kenya's population, are finding it difficult to cope and to relate to the Christianity of their parents, despite the fact that they go to church on Sunday. They still see fighting at home, they see protests led by politicians and tribal leaders, and they see hatred emanating from their community and against that community. Our young people are finding it difficult to relate to this faith that does not portray in practice what we say we believe in and what we read in the Bible. We have a big following of Christianity in Africa, but when it comes to practice and living out the Christian faith, it's a big challenge.

What opportunities do you think Christianity and the Church have among young adults in your country?

My struggle as the Archbishop of the Anglican Church of Kenya is how to create community around the Church—how to make the local church the symbol of mission where the church gathers people for worship, and then outside of normal church times convenes for Bible study and small groups. These discussions would cover topics we're all concerned about, such as bringing farmers together to talk about production of their farms or inviting young professionals to give back to society in terms of what they have acquired through their education and learning.

The Church still holds some level of trust, especially in Africa. We also need to be courageous enough to go to where people are, to introduce Christianity in the market and in the workplace so that when people are working, there is an opportunity for them to be able to know what God is saying to their life.

IN A MULTI-FAITH CONTEXT

DR. JAYAKUMAR CHRISTIAN
Author, theologian, former national director & CEO of World Vision India
INDIA

How do you see churches working to keep young Christians in the Church even after they leave home or start their own lives?

My church has been struggling with why we're not able to attract new young people into the Church. Our young people are drawn to strong, dynamic movements. In recent elections in India, millions were first-time voters. Every political party went after them, but the Church is unable to get a similar response, possibly because young people don't see the Church as relevant to the causes and issues that matter to them. We also have the complication of a lack of credible leadership within the Church. In a country that's looking for leaders, the Church is not able to provide an alternative.

I also think the Church is struggling with young people having access to information that many of the previous generations never had. It's just significantly complicated life and choices for the younger generation.

What are some obstacles that the Church and Christians face as a minority religion in India?

Many of those who belong to religious minorities experience living in fear. The political environment is not conducive for minority religions to flourish, and I know from a Christian or Muslim perspective, eviction, abuse and disenfranchisement are common fears. Religion has been used to divide, and "religion" for many is a bad word now.

What unique advantages or opportunities do you think Christianity and the Church have among young adults in your country?

There's a lot of good will for Christians in terms of social service. We've done good work, and we're known for caring, being respectful to class, color, creed and gender. We are known as people who have given our lives for the cause of the poor and the cause of the nation. I think the Church has a unique advantage because we offer a relationship; we don't offer a religion. ●

Conflicted Views of Christianity

THOUGH ATTITUDES TOWARD CHRISTIANITY ARE POSITIVE OVERALL,
THERE ARE SOME RESERVATIONS ABOUT THE RELIGION, IF NOT ABOUT
ITS MEMBERS

For church leaders, one of the welcome (and perhaps unexpected) findings of this report is the apparent openness that 18–35-year-olds feel toward spirituality and religion (see page 58). But does that warmth extend to Christianity specifically—even in an era when, as other Barna studies note, secularism is on the rise in some countries and many young Christians are reluctant to discuss faith?*

Generally, there is a (mostly) sunny outlook toward the Church in this study. Just about half of young adults say the Church is good for people (55%) and important to society (52%), far exceeding the roughly one in five who sees the institution as harmful to people (20%) or a detriment to society (22%). These proportions aren't quite as large as those who report similarly positive views of religion, broadly speaking, but still speak to approval of the Christian faith.

Depending on a young adult's personal religious context, however, this warm regard toward the Church sometimes cools.

*Barna has explored these themes in many studies over the years, mostly in the United States but also some European countries. Recent findings are available in Barna reports including *Reviving Evangelism*, *Spiritual Conversations in the Digital Age*, *The UK Church in Action*, *Finding Faith in Ireland* and *Transforming Scotland*.

Young Adults in Secularized Nations Still See the Church as Important

To some extent, views of the institutional Church may be shaped by the religious environment in which an 18–35-year-old lives. For instance, most young adults living in one of the 12 Christian nations in this survey describe the Church positively, as good for people (65% vs. 16% who say it's harmful) and important to society (63% vs. 18% who say it's detrimental). There are a number of reasons 18–35-year-olds in these contexts may have a favorable view of the pervasive religion of their nation, whether because they see Christianity as a common good or merely a cultural norm.

In other faith climates, even though there may not be a large Christian presence, there also seems to be a deep respect for the institutional Church. About half of the young adults in multi-faith contexts describe the Church as a force for good, for individuals or society (51% and 46%, respectively). Many also consider it a neutral presence, though three in 10 describe

ABOUT HALF OF YOUNG ADULTS SAY THE CHURCH IS GOOD FOR PEOPLE (49%) AND IMPORTANT TO SOCIETY (47%)

the Church as harmful to people or detrimental to society (14% and 15%, respectively).

In nations that could be regarded as having post-Christian or secular religious climates, responses are evenly distributed and closer to the average. This suggests *warm opinions of Christianity may linger even when an environment becomes irreligious,* pointing to the power of shared traditions and religious history. These young adults are still inclined to view the Church as both a personal good (45% vs. 26% who say it's harmful to people) and a public asset (40% vs. 30% who say it's detrimental to society).

IDEAS ABOUT CHRISTIAN IDENTITY, BY RELIGIOUS AFFILIATION

How do you know if someone is a Christian?

● Total ● Christians ● Other faith ○ No faith

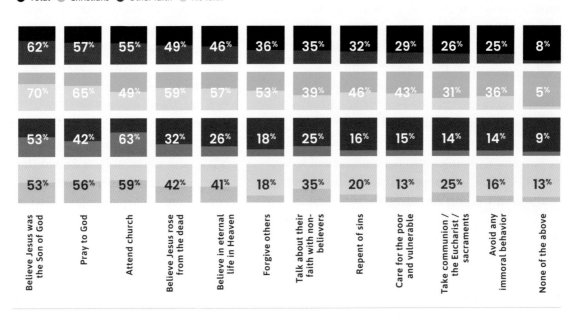

	Believe Jesus was the Son of God	Pray to God	Attend church	Believe Jesus rose from the dead	Believe in eternal life in Heaven	Forgive others	Talk about their faith with non-believers	Repent of sins	Care for the poor and vulnerable	Take communion / the Eucharist / sacraments	Avoid any immoral behavior	None of the above
Total	62%	57%	55%	49%	46%	36%	35%	32%	29%	26%	25%	8%
Christians	70%	65%	49%	59%	57%	53%	39%	46%	43%	31%	36%	5%
Other faith	53%	42%	63%	32%	26%	18%	25%	16%	15%	14%	14%	9%
No faith	53%	56%	59%	42%	41%	18%	35%	20%	13%	25%	16%	13%

n=15,369 adults ages 18 to 35, December 4, 2018–February 15, 2019.

The Church Has a (Mostly) Good Reputation

Zooming in from the national to the personal level, there are other patterns in young adults' perspectives of Christianity depending on their religious affiliation or practice.

The majority of Christian 18–35-year-olds is assured of the value of their religion (77% say it's good for people, 73% say it's important to society). Likewise, members of faiths other than Christianity tend to see the Church in a positive (49% say it's good for people, 45% say it's important to society) rather than negative light (18% harmful for people, 20% a detriment to society). Agnostics, atheists and those of no religion, however, are more skeptical of the Church's benefit (42% say it's harmful for people, 47% say it's a detriment to society).

Reviewing responses to a number of other possible descriptors for the Church—negative, neutral and positive—highlights some of the challenges facing the reputation of present-day Christianity. For instance, **though plenty of 18–35-year-olds say Christianity is a faith they respect (37% "a lot") and presents good values and principles (33% "a lot"), one-third describes it as "anti-homosexual" (32% "a lot").**

Naturally, the responses of Christians, especially those who are practicing, significantly buoys the sample's overall opinion of the Church as friendly, respected and loving. Though, as the chart details, believers seem willing to note some criticisms of Christianity as anti-homosexual, judgmental or hypocritical. Meanwhile, young adults without a religious faith—atheists, agnostics and "nones"—confidently back many of the negative statements about Christianity and express the least agreement with positive statements.

"Who Do You Say That I Am?"

This study looks at not only what 18–35-year-olds around the world believe about followers of Jesus, but also what they believe about Jesus himself. Who do they think Jesus is? Of several options presented, the most commonly chosen is "the Son of God" (57%). Roughly one-fifth calls him "a prophet" (23%), "a historical figure" (21%) or "a miracle worker" (20%). Christians overwhelmingly agree with his identity as God's Son (87%). Atheists, agnostics and those of no faith tend to see Jesus though a less divine, even fictional lens, as "a historical figure" (29%) or perhaps just "a character from a story" (28%) or "a myth / legend" (23%), though one in four still says he is "the Son of God" (24%). It's possible this reflects their recognition of how Jesus is regarded within the Christian faith rather than a statement they believe to be true.

YOUNG ADULTS BELIEVE THAT PRESENT-DAY CHRISTIANITY, TO SOME EXTENT, TEACHES THE SAME BASIC IDEAS AS OTHER RELIGIONS

Young adults who belong to other faiths, perhaps because they still carry an appreciation for religion, are less critical of the Church's nature. This could also stem from a general sense that Christian teachings aren't all that distinctive. Across a number of factors—including national religious climate, religious affiliation and even practicing faith— young adults believe that present-day Christianity, to some extent, teaches the same basic ideas as other religions (overall, 50% "some," 23% "a lot").

Non-Christians Identify Christians by Their Church Attendance

In John 13:35, Jesus says that people will know his followers because of their love. So, how do people today know someone is a Christian? What notions or defining traits come to mind when 18–35-year-olds think about members of the Church?

Overall, when respondents were asked to select among a list of qualities or behaviors, the three most frequently chosen indicators of Christian faith are a belief that Jesus is the Son of God (62%), a habit of praying to God (57%) and church at-tendance (55%). The least frequently chosen indicators include caring for the poor and vulnerable (29%), taking sacraments (26%) and avoiding immoral behavior (25%).

Christians themselves are eager to associate their fellows with all of the possible descriptions—with the notable exception of church attendance, which they are actually less likely than others to see as a marker of Christianity (49%, compared to 63% of members of other faiths and 59% of members of no faith). For these Christians, a concept of genuine faith goes beyond sitting in a service to a (largely internal) adherence to certain beliefs. *To those outside the Church, participation in a worship community is the benchmark of Christianity*, though there is still a widespread acknowledgment of Christians' core belief in Jesus as the Son of God.

However they recognize people of faith, non-Christians who personally know Christians believe good things about their faithful friends. The majority either holds a positive opinion (46%) or considers Christians to be no different than anyone else (40%), with only one in eight non-Christians (13%) expressing a negative opinion about a Christian peer. Those who practice another faith are exceptionally warm toward members of Christianity,

IDEAS ABOUT MODERN CHRISTIANITY, BY RELIGIOUS AFFILIATION

"Present-day Christianity ..."
% say "a lot" or "some"

● Total ◐ Christians ● Other faith ○ No faith

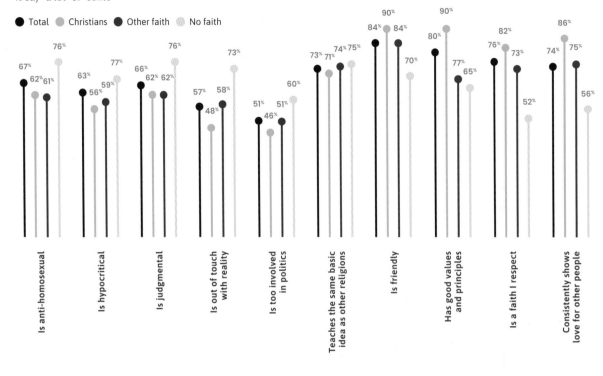

n=15,369 adults ages 18 to 35, December 4, 2018–February 15, 2019.

usually holding a positive (63%) or at least neutral (31%) view of these individuals.

With this generation's observed degree of warmth toward the Church, at large and especially one-on-one, there is reason to hope that—through personal relationships and the collective efforts of the Church—Christians can better communicate their distinguishing beliefs, expand the conception of their tradition (beyond church attendance alone) and cultivate a fuller understanding of the Christian life. ●

TO THOSE OUTSIDE THE CHURCH, PARTICIPATION IN A WORSHIP COMMUNITY IS THE BENCHMARK OF CHRISTIANITY

YOUNG ADULTS & CHRISTIANITY AROUND THE WORLD

CHRISTIAN PRESENCE ACROSS RELIGIOUS CLIMATES

● All Christians   ● Practicing Christians   ● Non-practicing Christians

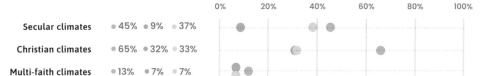

				0%	20%	40%	60%	80%	100%
Secular climates	● 45%	● 9%	● 37%						
Christian climates	● 65%	● 32%	● 33%						
Multi-faith climates	● 13%	● 7%	● 7%						

CHURCH ATTENDANCE

● All Christians   ● Practicing Christians

	Once a week or more	A few times a month	Once a month	A few times every six months	Once or twice a year	Less than once a year	Never	Do not attend a place of worship but used to	Do not attend a place of worship and never did
All Christians	71%	22%	7%						
Practicing Christians	33%	14%	7%	11%	12%	7%	4%	10%	1%

TOP 5 REASONS CHURCHGOING CHRISTIANS PARTICIPATE IN A COMMUNITY OF WORSHIP

% among Christians who have attended church in the past month

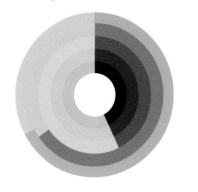

 67% To grow in my faith

 65% To learn about God

 43% For teachings that are relevant to my life

 43% Because it is how I live out my faith

 43% For wisdom for how to live faithfully

DISCIPLINES & BELIEFS

● All Christians   ● Practicing Christians

DONATIONS *% give at least monthly to ...*

	All Christians	Practicing Christians
Their community of worship	● 28%	● 50%
A local charity	● 17%	● 23%
An international charity	● 9%	● 11%
A Christian charity	● 16%	● 27%

CHRISTIAN PRACTICES *% report doing the following at least monthly*

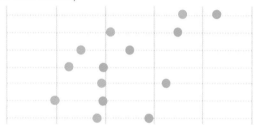

	All Christians	Practicing Christians
Pray on my own	● 72%	● 86%
Pray with others	● 42%	● 70%
Tell others about my beliefs	● 30%	● 50%
Volunteer my time	● 25%	● 39%
Read scripture on my own	● 38%	● 65%
Attend a small group or a scripture study	● 19%	● 39%
Read books about faith or religious topics	● 37%	● 59%

DIGITAL DISCIPLINES *% report doing the following at least monthly*

	All Christians	Practicing Christians
Watch religious speakers or teachers (on videos or TV broadcasts)	● 30%	● 52%
Listen to faith or religious speakers or teachers (on podcasts or radio broadcasts)	● 30%	● 52%
Listen to or sing worship music	● 46%	● 73%
Share or read religious teachings on social media	● 31%	● 51%

FAITH STATEMENTS *% strongly agree*

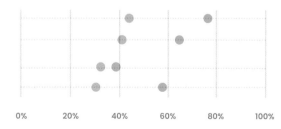

	All Christians	Practicing Christians
"The Bible is totally accurate in all of the principles it teaches"	● 44%	● 77%
"When I die, I will go to heaven because I have confessed my sins and have accepted Jesus Christ as my savior"	● 41%	● 65%
"People can earn heaven through good works"	● 32%	● 39%
"I have a personal responsibility to tell other people about my religious beliefs"	● 30%	● 58%

n=15,369 adults ages 18 to 35 (including 7,687 who identify as Christian), December 4, 2018–February 15, 2019.
See page 12 or barna.com/glossary for all definitions.

Q & A

The Growth of Pentecostalism

The Pentecostal Church has been growing at much quicker rates than other denominations in parts of Africa.[21] Why do you think that is?

The preaching and demonstration of the power of the Holy Spirit is at the center of the growth of Pentecostalism. These demonstrations of the power of God through tangible miracles and healings serve to show that God is real.

What is it about the community, teaching or worship expression that you think connects with young adults?

The dynamism of the preaching and teaching of the gospel, as opposed to rote liturgy (which unfortunately has become the norm in mainline denominations) has been especially attractive to young people. Millennials tend to identify with the informality of the services, devoid of strict liturgy and set vestments. Most services incorporate up to 30 minutes of dynamic worship with contemporary music. This is followed by or supplemented with other forms, such as drama, spoken word, dance and choreography. A relevant Bible teaching or preaching follows, crowned with a time for ministry to the people, such as an altar call for salvation, prayers for the sick or prayers for those with needs.

We see a general openness toward spiritual forces and faith among 18–35-year-olds. Does this surprise you?

Many people, whether Christian or not, are becoming more aware of spiritual powers and forces. When the Church does not address these fears, concerns or needs, people tend to turn to witchcraft, the occult and other forms of spiritism.

More than 60 percent of young adults in Kenya attend church weekly, and three-quarters believe the Christian Church is good for people and important to society. Why do you think young adults in Kenya are so drawn to the Church?

We could be reaping from the East Africa Revival of the 1960s and 70s when there was a major move of the Holy Spirit. This resulted in many people turning to the Pentecostal movement, especially in schools and colleges. The children of these converts are young adults today. In all probability, they are walking in the faith of their parents, but also finding God for themselves. The flexibility of the Pentecostal charismatic churches has also given them room for self-expression of their faith in a contemporary manner. ●

REV. DAVID OGINDE, PHD
Presiding Bishop of Christ Is the
Answer Ministries (CITAM)
KENYA

Q & A

Connecting Through Worship

As you look into the crowds that you lead in worship, what do you sense about this generation? What are they longing for?

There is no counterfeit for the presence of God. I think young people today are leaning in more than ever to worship. They recognize a shift when people come together. I've noticed in certain worship gatherings when you can sense the faith and expectation in the room, the atmosphere shifts and things that could otherwise take years to break off or leave behind are broken in a moment. There is freedom in worship—and who doesn't want to be free?

Why do you believe worship—especially corporate worship—plays such a special role in people's faith?

Worship takes our eyes off of ourselves and places our focus and adoration on Jesus. Worship reminds us of who God is, who he says we are and what he has done. It is a great privilege to place sound and scriptural theology in the mouths of young people through our music.

Do you see a connection between young adults' spiritual openness and the culture Hillsong has created?

It could be said that everyone is in pursuit of truth. The state of the world and the sadness and desperation we are exposed to daily through media and online engagement only heighten our awareness of our own need. Young people don't want to be impressed; they want something real, lasting.

I love that my church has a culture of "welcome home." At any [Hillsong] campus, you will sense the same "come as you are" love and embrace, an authenticity that genuinely loves people just as they are, believing that when they find a relationship with God and get grounded in authentic community, their lives will always change for the better.

How have you seen worship music break cultural barriers?

I think the role of music and worship is to do what it has always done: engage, remind, encourage, uplift, put our focus on and attention toward God. Music is a gift, as it has the ability to go where our literal selves can not, opens people who might otherwise be closed off and speaks where words fail. It is a universal language that cuts through even religious obstacles and cynical thinking. We need worshippers in every genre of music to reach every person possible with the gospel message of Jesus. ●

TAYA SMITH
Worship leader for Hillsong United
AUSTRALIA

The Continued Impact of Teen Faith

YOUNG ADULTS WHO WERE VERY ACTIVE IN THEIR FAITH IN
ADOLESCENCE OFTEN EXPERIENCE LONGEVITY AND DEPTH OF BELIEF

Church leaders longing to understand the religious profile of today's young adults may need to start with yesterday's teens. Most 18–35-year-olds who grew up religious weren't just along for the ride; two-thirds indicate that, during their teen years (for some, a not-so-distant memory), they were actively engaged in the faith of their upbringing (27% very + 40% somewhat active). Further, this experience usually correlates with clinging to one's faith into adulthood; most of those who were very actively religious in their teens (87%) have neither changed nor left that religion, with small percentages saying they switched (6%) or abandoned (6%) faith at some point down the road. Meanwhile, a much higher percentage of those who were inactive in their faith as a teen (23%) have gone on to leave religion entirely.

This trend holds when looking at Christians specifically. Most of the respondents who have always been Christian were at least somewhat active in practicing their faith as a teenager (32% very + 41% somewhat active). This is especially true of those who regularly attend church and highly value their faith today (53% of practicing Christians were very active in their teenage faith).

Of course, teenage faithfulness isn't always a guarantee of lifelong commitment; nearly half of young adults who have left the Christian Church still report having been active in their faith during their teen years (14% very + 32% somewhat active). Looking at those who are no longer Chris-

MOST OF THE RESPONDENTS WHO HAVE ALWAYS BEEN CHRISTIAN WERE AT LEAST SOMEWHAT ACTIVE IN PRACTICING THEIR FAITH AS A TEENAGER

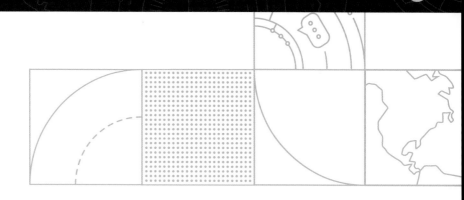

TEENAGE FAITH ACTIVITY & LONGEVITY OF FAITH

● Very active faith
○ Somewhat active teen faith
◐ Inactive teen faith

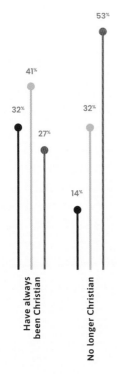

n=9,502 adults age 18 to 35 who were Christians in their upbringing, December 4, 2018–February 5, 2019.

tians, there's a general antagonism toward their late faith (see page 89)—however, divide this group to study those who had a high level of faith engagement in their teen years, and you'll find a remnant of reverence toward the Church. They are more likely than former Christians whose teenage roots weren't as strong to continue to call Christianity good for people (34% vs. 25%), important to society (31% vs. 19%) and a faith they personally respect (20% vs. 11% "a lot"). They also more readily identify Jesus as the Son of God (41% vs. 29%). Some aspects of their youthful devotion or theological understanding seem to stick with them even after their religious identity has shifted or faded.

Traits of Continued Commitment

Looking at 18–35-year-olds who have always been Christian, those who were more enthusiastic about their religious practice in their teens show greater conviction surrounding certain faith statements. These active respondents are often about twice as likely to strongly agree with tenets such as the Bible's total accuracy (52% vs. 24% of those who have always been Christian but weren't active in their faith during their teen years), salvation and eternal life through Jesus Christ (47% vs. 25%) and a responsibility to share one's religious beliefs with others (36% vs. 15%). Affirming that their relationship with Jesus brings them great joy (61% vs. 32% strongly agree), they are more likely than Christians whose

CHRISTIANS WITH FERVENT TEENAGE FAITH EXPERIENCES ARE EXPONENTIALLY MORE LIKELY THAN OTHER LIFELONG BELIEVERS TO NURTURE THEIR ADULT FAITH

faith was inactive during their youth to say they hope Jesus is reflected through their words and actions (56% vs. 28%).

Though this study doesn't cover what behaviors, exactly, respondents associate with having been very active Christians in their teens, it does speak to their various spiritual disciplines in the present. In many cases, Christians with fervent teenage faith experiences are exponentially more likely than other lifelong believers to nurture their adult faith. This begins with church attendance, which is the norm for this group of Christians who look back on a faithful youth (39% vs. 16% who attend at least once a week). Beyond services, these Christians' monthly habits indicate a robust personal and corporate spiritual practice, whether praying on their own (77% vs. 58%) or with others (50% vs. 23%), reading scripture (44% vs. 22%), giving money to places of worship (33% vs. 15%) or attending small groups (23% vs. 9%). They seek out other ways of growing spiritually through media, particularly worship music (53% vs. 27%) and books about faith (44% vs. 22%).

As in other points of this research, the presence of a spiritual network—both then and now—is a factor in depth of discipleship. Lifelong Christians whose faith was already highly engaged in their teens often report having had church friends of older generations during their upbringing (40% vs. 15% of those who have always been Christian but weren't active in their faith during their teen years strongly agree),

and more than half can point to a present relationship that encourages their spiritual growth today (53% vs. 29% strongly agree). Further, spirituality in youth correlates with sensitivity and generosity toward one's community in adulthood; a majority of these Christians senses a call to give of their time to help people (61% vs. 44%), be concerned about others' welfare (59% vs. 48%) and stand up against injustice (51% vs. 41%) and corruption (51% vs. 38%).

Teenage faith activity is clearly impactful (yes, even when left behind). However the seeds of adolescent faith are watered—by one's environment, religious climate, church teaching, relationships or personal diligence—the data underscore the importance of focusing on developing young disciples who will take ownership of their Christian identity for the long term.

The Role of Relationships in Faith Formation

LASTING, ENGAGED FAITH IS LINKED TO HAVING SPIRITUALLY SUPPORTIVE COMMUNITY

"As iron sharpens iron, so a friend sharpens a friend," scripture tells us—and this study speaks to the truth of that Proverb.

Among 18–35-year-olds who identify as Christians, close to half (46%) strongly agree there is someone in their life who encourages them to grow spiritually. Another third (32%) somewhat agrees with this statement—meaning, however, that a little more than one-fifth (22%) lacks this kind of relational and faith support.

Having a spiritual mentor or encourager is more common among practicing Christians (73% vs. 29% of non-practicing

Christians), and those who say they have always been Christians are more likely than those who came to the faith later (46% vs. 34%) to acknowledge a spiritual mentor. This could be due to the fact that they've had more time to establish meaningful connections in their faith community. As suggested in the previous article, there may be ties between longevity of faith and the spiritual encouragement of others, particularly during one's formative years. For instance, those who know someone who supports them in their spiritual development are more likely than other Christians to have been very active in their faith as a teen (36% vs. 16%). Further, four in 10 of those Christians who have spiritual encour-

TEENAGE FAITH ACTIVITY & SPIRITUAL GUIDES
% strongly agree

● Very active teen faith   ● Inactive teen faith

"There is someone in my life who encourages my spiritual growth"

65%
30%

"Growing up, I had adult friends at church"

55%
15%

n=7,463 adults ages 18 to 35 who identify as Christian, December 4, 2018–February 15, 2019.

agers today (40% strongly agree) look back on having had adult friends in their church while growing up (compared to 10% among Christians who don't know someone who presently supports their spiritual growth).

Having guides in one's faith journey correlates with a number of positive experiences or traits. Eighteen to 35-year-old Christians who presently know someone who encourages them spiritually are also more likely to express optimism about the future, feel able to accomplish goals or recognize someone who believes in them. Compared to Christians without a friend who champions their discipleship, they feel a deeper connection to the world (64% vs. 45%) and events within it (82% vs. 70%). Spiritually, they have good things to say about religion in general, the Church at large as well as their own local church, in which they are more likely to find everything from opportunities to serve the poor to leadership training. These trends are more subtle but still apparent among those who had multi-generational community at church in their youth.

The data can't show which comes first: Are spiritually supportive friends a byproduct of strong faith and faith communities? Or do such relationships truly reinforce one's ties to both Christianity and church? What is clear is that, for the young adults around the world who cling to Christianity, there is a powerful communal aspect to personal spiritual development. ●

SPIRITUAL GUIDES & CHURCH EXPERIENCES

"Which of the following, if any, have you experienced in your church, parish or faith community?"

● Christians who have a spiritual encourager
● Christians who do not have a spiritual encourager

46%	29%	I have learned what it feels like to be part of a team
43%	24%	I have been inspired to live generously
43%	33%	I am given real chances to contribute to my church
40%	25%	My church has helped me better understand the needs of the poor
34%	24%	I have had the opportunity to serve the poor in my community
33%	23%	My church has helped me better understand what's happening for the poor globally
33%	17%	My church has helped me better understand the needs of marginalized people
32%	20%	My church has helped me better understand social justice
28%	17%	I have found a cause or issue I'm passionate about
27%	12%	I have been inspired to be a leader
24%	13%	I have had an adult mentor at church, other than the pastor or church staff
22%	11%	I have access to leadership training for ministry
21%	14%	I have taken a trip that broadened my understanding of the world
20%	8%	I have been inspired to be a missionary
6%	17%	None

n=4,091 adults ages 18 to 35 who identify as Christian and attend church at least every six months, December 4, 2018–February 15, 2019.

A Profile of Committed Catholics

TAKING A CLOSER LOOK AT A DEVOTED
MINORITY IN A RELIGIOUS COMMUNITY
UNDERGOING SEISMIC CHANGE

In this study, a sizeable proportion of 18–35-year-olds is influenced by, if not a current member of, the Catholic community. One-third of the sample lives in a nation where Catholicism is the primary religious presence. Today, one in four respondents (24%) identifies as Catholic—though one-third says they had a Catholic upbringing (33%). Catholics, even if only in identity and not in regular practice, are still just as common in post-Christian or seular climates as Christian ones (27% each), speaking to the Catholic Church's strong hold even in secularizing contexts.

Comparing former and current religious affiliation, however, shows a dramatic shift in Catholicism. We see this particularly among residents of Latin and South American nations included in this survey; though 63 percent of young adults in these regions say they grew up Catholic, less than half (47%) identify as such today. Meanwhile, among young adults who now identify as atheist, agnostic or irreligious, one in four (23%) considers themselves a former Catholic. These statistics track with other records that show notable declines not only in membership, but in the priesthood, especially in the wake of institutional scandals.[22] Rates of weekly attendance in North America and Western Europe continue to track downward.[23] At the same time, some regions, like sub-Saharan Africa, are seeing a surge in Catholic adherents, and there are even striking examples of a growing, diverse group of American Millennials who aspire to become Catholic sisters.[24]

Clearly, Catholicism is at yet another complex turning point in its long history. And in looking at the Christian expression of 18–35-year-olds in 25 countries, we have an opportunity to create a unique faith profile of Catholics across geographies and cultures—and to learn what drives some of the most active participants in the Catholic Church today.

What Motivates Catholics Who Regularly Attend Services?

Just over one-fifth of self-identified Catholic adults in this study (22%) reports attending a religious service weekly. Another quarter says they attend a few times (16%) or once (8%) a month. Most have more sporadic attendance habits, with 17 percent indicating they do not attend services outside weddings or funerals.

Given the centrality of the mass and Eucharist in Catholic tradition, these attendance rates seem quite low, and on many measures Catholics' enthusiasm for church engagement lags behind their Protestant peers (44% of whom attend services at least once a week). Even in Christian climates, weekly attendance among Catholics climbs only to

31 percent. But what can we learn from the minority of Catholics in this age group who participate in their churches with great frequency? And in what other ways are they present and practicing throughout the week?

The overwhelming majority of Catholics, regardless of current involvement with the Church or their religious climate, says they were raised in their denomination—but **those who attend weekly stand out in that they were also "very active" in their faith as teens (52% vs. 27% of all Catholics) and still regard their faith as "very important" (77% vs. 53%).** Today, they are primarily motivated to participate in church to "grow in their faith" (65% vs. 53% of all Catholics) and "learn about God" (62% vs. 49%). Forty-three percent say involvement in a worship community is central to their faith practice; it's how they "live out their faith." Through it, they hope to gain "teachings that are relevant to life" (40% vs. 29%) or "wisdom to live faithfully" (38% vs. 27%) and "apply scripture to life" (34% vs. 22%). Specific aspects of the service are also more important to these Catholics, such as worship music (32% vs. 22%), prayer events (32% vs. 22%) and sacraments (31% vs. 22%). Outside of mass, regular attendees remain prayerful and are more likely to study scripture than their peers who attend less often.

So what might hold back 18–35-year-olds who embrace a more nominal expression of their Catholic faith? Among those

COMMUNITY IS CRUCIAL FOR CATHOLICS WHO REGULARLY ATTEND CHURCH

who identify as Catholic but infrequently or never attend services, barriers relate to the Church's reputation, as shown in strong resistance to politicization (80% who never attend, 75% who infrequently attend) and corruption in the Church (74% and 69%, respectively). Many also see flaws in church teachings (70% and 62%, respectively). Overall, more than three-quarters of Catholics who have some connection to Christianity but never attend church (77%) say it's simply not an essential part of their faith—similar to the percentage of weekly attendees who disagree with this statement (79%).

A Collective Effort
Community is crucial for Catholics who regularly attend church. About one in four self-identified Catholics—regardless of the frequency with which they attend services—says they participate in church to be involved in a community or to attend alongside family. They also all agree on the main thing missing from their experiences at church: friends. Still, two-thirds of weekly attenders (66%) enjoy the company of someone who encourages their spiritual growth. These encouraging relationships set apart these more-involved Catholics in secular cultures; 61 percent know someone who encourages their spiritual growth, compared to just 16 percent of those who attend infrequently or never in a post-Christian or secular religious climate.

The power of such community crosses denominational lines: Similar proportions of Protestants who attend church regularly also benefit from spiritually supportive friendships (73%).

There are some signs of a sense of duty among engaged Catholics, who see church attendance as one of the top ways to identify a Christian (61%). But **weekly attendees also report being part of dynamic communities of faith that involve them as members and harness their passion for justice.** Through their participation in church, they feel inspired to live generously (42% vs. 30% of less frequent Catholic attendees) and gain a better understanding of the needs of the poor (42% vs. 27%) and marginalized (34% vs. 24%), who they are given opportunities to serve locally (34% vs. 24%). They feel like teammates (41% vs. 30%) and see chances to contribute at church (37% vs. 27%). Empowered with a better understanding of their purpose (62% vs. 52%), they are better helped to live out their faith in the workplace, too (42% vs. 33%).

This study can't say whether these Catholics attend more often because of these positive environments, or if these are some of the benefits of first being more present in a faith community—but the data show that, across religious climates, these are the pronounced experiences of young Catholics who interact with their places of worship frequently and fervently. ●

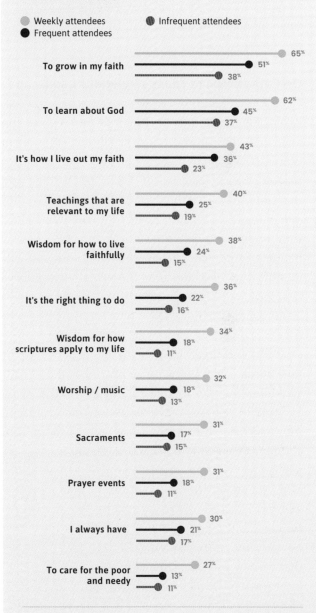

TOP REASONS CATHOLICS ENGAGE WITH THE CHURCH

"Why do you participate in your community of worship?" Select all that apply.

● Weekly attendees   ◗ Infrequent attendees
● Frequent attendees

To grow in my faith
65%
51%
38%

To learn about God
62%
45%
37%

It's how I live out my faith
43%
36%
23%

Teachings that are relevant to my life
40%
25%
19%

Wisdom for how to live faithfully
38%
24%
15%

It's the right thing to do
36%
22%
16%

Wisdom for how scriptures apply to my life
34%
18%
11%

Worship / music
32%
18%
13%

Sacraments
31%
17%
15%

Prayer events
31%
18%
11%

I always have
30%
21%
17%

To care for the poor and needy
27%
13%
11%

n=2,196 Catholics ages 18 to 35 who attend church at least a few times every six months, December 4, 2018–February 15, 2019.

Q & A

The Future of the Catholic Church

On Catholicism in Today's Religious Landscape

FR. MARCO: Latin American countries have always been religious. Its inhabitants are sensitive to religion / spirituality, and our social, cultural and even political practices are highly influenced by this. Of course, having been colonized by European political powers, self-professed Catholic countries at that time, the role of the Catholic Church in the construction of our countries and our culture has been indeed important. The relationship between Church and state was and still is intrinsic. Although the majority of Latin Americans still identifies as Catholic, over the years, especially since the last decade of the 20th century, the religious landscape has evolved and is more varied.

FR. PETER: Several things bring young people to the Catholic Church. First, is the sense of tradition and history. The Catholic Church is founded on scripture (the Word of God) and tradition (the Apostolic tradition), and young people are intrigued by a Church that has an unbroken tradition of proclaiming Jesus Christ. Second, as Catholics, we believe that when we pray, we are not only joined by those around us but also by a great communion of saints, holy men and women who preceded us on the journey to God and who intercede for us. Many young adults appreciate the idea that we cannot only ask our family and friends to pray for us to God, but that we can also ask saints to join our prayer and offer their intercession. Third, young people appreciate the sacrament of reconciliation. As a priest, I live in a part of the city that is super young. Every week I hear confessions, and I am always amazed by a long line of people in their 20s, waiting to receive this special grace. I take great hope in that movement as it reveals that a growing number of young adults are tired of being self-justified and now seek God's mercy, God's grace and God's help to overcome their struggle and grow in holiness.

On Drawing Young People Toward the Life of the Church

FR. MARCO: If they see that faith and church participation connect to real life issues and aim to contribute in solving them—especially in countries where the political environment is clouded with authoritarianism, a decline in participatory democracy and the right to speak out—they will engage in a more genuine and enthusiastic way in church life. I see them participating in activities that put them in contact and in service to the poor or the marginalized of our societies. I see them active in advocacy efforts to bring justice to unjust situations. Their participation in liturgy, often seen as boring, unnecessary and outdated, will be more active, more conscious and joyful, as it will mean something more than bench-warming. They will then feel eager to know more about the fundamentals of faith and begin a process of formation.

FR. JAMES: There's never been a more difficult time for teenagers to try to be faithful. Churches should aim for the parents. If you start building a culture of evangeliz-ing parents, then there's a whole group of young people that are going to grow up in a different environment. From there, young people who are exposed not only to their parents, but also to their parents' peers who have an authentic, living faith and to people their own age who have a faith—these are the relationships that will help bring young people to church and keep them there.

On Repairing the Damage of Abuse & Scandal

FR. MARCO: The sex abuse scandals among priests and other church officials has hurt the fundamental basis of trust in those who lead. Of course, there is a sense of deceit and profound disapproval, as the issue is fundamentally a matter of justice. Much needs to be done, but the Catholic Church has started to take steps. The first one is to acknowledge that abuse has been happening, it has been covered up systematically, and something needs to be done to put an end to it.

FATHER JAMES MALLON
Founder of Divine Renovation,
Episcopal Vicar for Parish Renewal and
leadership support for the Archdiocese
of Halifax-Yarmouth, Nova Scotia
CANADA

FATHER PETER WOJCIK
Director of the Department
of Parish Vitality and
Mission at Archdiocese
of Chicago
UNITED STATES

FATHER MARCO TULIO GÓMEZ, S.J.
Jesuit priest and anthropologist,
executive secretary of the
International Federation
of Fe y Alegría
COLOMBIA

There is a serious effort to identify the sources of abuse and to promote the creation and sustainment of a culture of protection and well-being for children, adolescents and vulnerable adults. Albeit, one would want all of this to be more widespread; there is still a sense of lag and lack of effective response to end this evil.

FR. PETER: One of the most critical things that the Catholic communities have to do is be clear about the progress we have made over the last years when it comes to the safety of children in our churches. I think young people want to make sure that we are open, honest and clear about what was done wrong, who committed the crime and what's our way forward. Another important element of moving forward is to ensure that our leadership in the Church is diversified and reflects both men and women, taking on ordained and lay leadership roles and keeping each other accountable. I am blessed to work in Chicago where we not only put those words to action but also attracted a good number of young people to work with us as leaders in a number of ministries of the Archdiocese.

On Openness to the Church in the Connected Generation

FR. MARCO: There is an openness to be and to let others be who they want to be. In this sense, most young adults have a respect for what others believe, particularly when they see a true and honest effort to be coherent with those beliefs. Non-Christians in Latin America still live and develop in a mostly Christian society. They chose not to adhere to organized religion or practices, but that does not mean they are disconnected from it entirely. They per-

ceive honesty and truth when they see it in acts, not words. In countries where the Catholic Church has been active and vocal in regard to denouncing injustice, non-Christians tend to appreciate and value it. It is common to hear, "I do not believe in religion, but I show my respect, and hats off to those who fight for justice."

FR. JAMES: Millennials aren't going to respond to some mass appeal, some big campaign. It's going to be rooted in relationships and friendship. We're seeing young people who had no background in the Church encountering the Lord and having an experience of God's love and friendship, and then saying, "Okay, now I'm willing to look at this Church thing." They may still struggle, they might have issues, they might think the Church is crazy on this issue or that issue, but they're willing to look at it.

FR. PETER: As St. Augustine said, our hearts long for God and are restless without him. Young people are not any different than the people of the past. They want to have big dreams, build successful lives and love with all their hearts. They also know there is more to life than this, and Christianity—or more importantly, life in Jesus—gives us the answer. I do think that young people, both in [my former home of] Poland and the U.S., are attracted by authenticity, holiness and natural goodness. Holiness attracts. Hence, Christianity will always attract people. ●

From the Outside Looking Back

18–35-YEAR-OLDS WHO HAVE LEFT
CHRISTIANITY HAVE HARSH VIEWS OF
THE FAITH—SOMETIMES MORE SO THAN
THOSE WHO HAVE NEVER BEEN A PART
OF IT

One of the main findings of this research is that 18–35-year-olds around the world are generally warm toward faith, including Christianity, even if they are not religiously engaged themselves. Standing in contrast, however, are young adults who grew up Christian but no longer identify with the religion (a group referred to by David Kinnaman as "Prodigals," as covered on page 95). Instead, they hold extreme stances against the Christian faith. In fact, they often express similar or even more negative ideas about the Church than do young adults who have never had personal connections to it.

Just 13 percent of the 18–35-year-olds in this study fall into this segment of former Christians, and they tend to live in countries with post-Christian / secular or Christian climates. Their **departure from Christianity rarely leads them to another faith;** today, this group usually identifies as not religious (47%), atheist (18%) or agnostic (17%). Half (51%) strongly

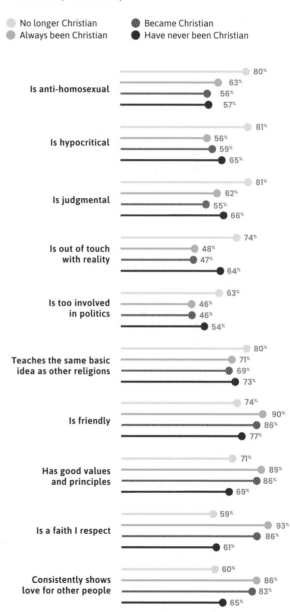

THOSE WHO HAVE LEFT CHRISTIANITY HAVE LOW OPINIONS OF THE CHURCH
"Present-day Christianity ..."

- No longer Christian
- Always been Christian
- Became Christian
- Have never been Christian

Is anti-homosexual
- 80%
- 63%
- 56%
- 57%

Is hypocritical
- 81%
- 56%
- 59%
- 65%

Is judgmental
- 81%
- 62%
- 55%
- 66%

Is out of touch with reality
- 74%
- 48%
- 47%
- 64%

Is too involved in politics
- 63%
- 46%
- 46%
- 54%

Teaches the same basic idea as other religions
- 80%
- 71%
- 69%
- 73%

Is friendly
- 74%
- 90%
- 86%
- 77%

Has good values and principles
- 71%
- 89%
- 86%
- 69%

Is a faith I respect
- 59%
- 93%
- 86%
- 61%

Consistently shows love for other people
- 60%
- 86%
- 83%
- 65%

n=15,369 adults ages 18 to 35, December 4, 2018–February 15, 2019.

disagree that religious faith is very important to them now.

Four in 10 of these no-longer-Christians are reluctant to say they still hold respect for the Christian faith (41% vs. 39% of young adults who have never been Christians say "not very much") or that it shows love for others (40% vs. 35% "not very much"). Similar proportions say the Church is actually a detriment to society (43% vs. 33%) or harmful to people (40% vs. 29%).

Other responses from church dropouts offer some clues as to why these adverse feelings exist. A strong majority says they want to distance themselves from the politics of the Church (89%) and that the institution is corrupt (85%). Six in 10 say the Church (61% "definitely not" + "probably not") doesn't make a difference when it comes to issues related to poverty and justice. And—much more than those who have never been Christian—*those who have left Christianity see it as hypocritical* (46% vs. 29% of those who've never been Christians), anti-homosexual (44% vs. 30%), judgmental (44% vs. 26%), too involved in politics (32% vs. 20%) and out of touch with reality (32% vs. 22%).

Given that these young adults say their beliefs just don't align with church teachings (84%), it's not surprising they also diverge in their perceptions of Jesus. Though about one-third calls him "the Son of God" (35%), those who have left Christianity are more likely than those with other experiences of Christianity to describe Jesus outside of a divine context, preferring to see him as "a historical figure" (35% vs. 19% of adults who have always been Christian, 22% of adults who have become Christian, 19% of adults who have never been Chris-

tian), "just a man" (26% vs. 5%, 8%, 19%), "a myth / legend" (21% vs. 4%, 9%, 16%) or even "a character from a story" (27% vs. 6%, 10%, 18%).

As much of this group is now irreligious, there are predictable dips in their likelihood of participating in spiritual disciplines, whether reading scripture (8% vs. 24% of all 18–35-year-olds), volunteering (17% vs. 22%), praying on their own (25% vs. 51%) or with others (9% vs. 29%).

There are some signs that, though they've separated from the religion, *these once-Christians have not cut off all ties to their former faith community.* Even with the unfavorable feelings mentioned above, a majority in this group (88%) still knows someone who practices Christianity—and for the most part, they hold positive (44%) or at least friendly (40% "neutral") views of these individuals. Interestingly, though many think they do not fit in at church (76%) and that it's difficult to connect with people there (70%), some still say they may become more active in church later in life (33%).

Should they return, these former Christians will be looking for substance. As it is, they are more likely than young adults who have always been outside the Church to see flaws or gaps in Christian teachings (86% vs. 74%), which they believe cannot address their questions (81% vs. 71%), their day-to-day life (79% vs. 68%) or real issues in society (69% vs. 65%). ●

Q & A

Making a Case for Church

Many young adults say they don't attend church because they find God elsewhere. What's your response to that?

The notion of that question is that church is a place we go to have God dispensed to us, as individuals. Of course, you can meet God in everyday life—that's never been disputed by anyone in the Church. Yet, there's a presumption that church is about my individual spiritual experience or encounter, which is just simply not what church is.

The Church is a family, and it's a communion around Jesus. The gospel is not an individual gospel where we're each called to Jesus and hope to meet him individually. We do that as a body; the Holy Spirit came to a body, to a group of people. If the Church is part of the gospel, if it's an institution that God has built and is calling us into, then the Church isn't just about my own individual needs being met. It's about this feast, particularly around Word and sacrament.

There's no other place you can go to receive the Word and the sacraments. The Church is coming together to meet Jesus together. Not just with our self-selection of friends and community that we like, but as part of this ancient and global community of Jesus.

How can churches intentionally lead young adults to practice daily rhythms through which they engage God?

People need to learn the story of scripture, the doctrines of the Church. There needs to be rich, solid teaching on theology and on practices. That's what people are yearning for. Church can't just be putting information in people's heads. There has to be a sense of practice of the way that Christians live—of how we use our time, our bodies, our money. All of that has to be deeply, theologically rooted in this broader story of what God is doing through time, so it doesn't seem like arbitrary rules, but something that is an invitation into the very heart of God.

Things like small groups have been important in our church in terms of growth and connection. The other thing that our church does is that every single person who goes through confirmation is paired with two mentors. You meet with them a few times over several months, talk, get to know each other, ask questions. You can wrestle with things. The whole life of the church, this person is a sponsor to them, a mentor to them. There's just no way to program spiritual growth—it's always going to have roots in relationships. You can't make relationships flourish, but I think you can create a culture where that's happening. •

TISH HARRISON WARREN
Anglican priest, author
UNITED STATES

What Draws Christians to Church?

YOUNG ADULTS WHO ATTEND CHURCH ARE MAINLY
THERE TO LEARN ABOUT FAITH AND GOD—BUT
THEY WISH THEIR FRIENDS JOINED THEM

Just over half of 18–35-year-old Christians in this study (54%) attend church at least once a month, including one-third (33%) who are in the pews once a week or more. Three in 10 (30%) attend less frequently. A small group of Christians (10%) says they used to go to church, but no longer do.

Despite their fairly consistent presence in the pews, almost half of Christians (44%) say that attending church is not an essential part of their faith. Practicing Christians, defined in part by their regular attendance, are less likely to feel this way, though one-fifth in this group (21%) still agrees. But even if belonging to a community of worship isn't always seen as essential, young *Christians who attend church point to many reasons their participation may be fruitful, most of which pertain to personal spiritual development.*

Church Is Primarily Seen as a Place to Grow Spiritually

About six in 10 Christians in this study say they participate in their community of worship to grow in their faith (63%) and learn about God (61%). These two options are by far the top responses, though other main motivations also relate to learning, such as receiving relevant teachings (40%), wisdom for how to live faithfully (39%) or wisdom for applying scriptures (35%). This desire for spiritual instruction persists even though four in 10 Christians in this age group (39%) say they have already learned most of what they need to know about faith, and nearly half (47%) say church teachings have flaws or gaps. (Interestingly, among those who have left the Christian faith, negative feelings emphasize the quality of teaching, which a majority in this group sees as irrelevant or unable to address their questions or daily lives. See page 89 for more about this group of church dropouts.)

For some, aspects of the service or liturgy stand out as reasons to engage with a faith community. More than one-third (37%) says they attend for the worship and music—though this is a more popular answer among Protestant respondents (50% Protestants vs. 22% of Catholics). On the other hand, sacraments (selected by 14% of all Christians) receive more emphasis among Catholics' responses (22% vs. 7% of Protestants). (Read more about how Catholic respondents relate to the Church on page 83.) These groups are similarly likely to see readings and recitations (15% of all Christians) as a driver for their church participation.

Some motivations for attending church speak to a sense of obligation or discipline. Four in 10 (40%) say church attendance is how they live out their faith, and one-third (33%) feels it's just the right thing to do. One in five notes that they participate in church because of their family (20%) or for their children (18%).

Young Christians Would Like More Company at Church

What do 18–35-year-old Christians who attend church wish was a part of their worship community? Encouragingly, when asked to identify from a list what might be missing from their church, the plurality response (20%) is "none of the above." However, nearly one-fifth (18%) says their friends are absent from their church experience. This may be partly due to the fact that religious affiliation and engagement has generally declined among younger

WHY CHRISTIANS GO TO CHURCH

"Why do you participate in your community of worship?"

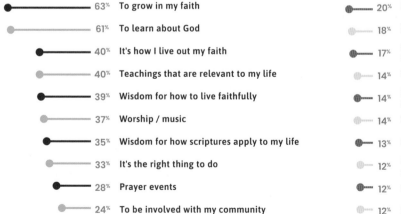

%	
63%	To grow in my faith
61%	To learn about God
40%	It's how I live out my faith
40%	Teachings that are relevant to my life
39%	Wisdom for how to live faithfully
37%	Worship / music
35%	Wisdom for how scriptures apply to my life
33%	It's the right thing to do
28%	Prayer events
24%	To be involved with my community

... AND WHAT THEY WISH THEY'D FIND THERE

"What do you think is missing from your community of worship?"

%	
20%	None of the above
18%	My friends attending
17%	Opportunities to fight injustice and oppression
14%	Vocational training
14%	Social gatherings outside of the worship space
14%	Workshops for strengthening relationships
13%	Support groups for challenges in my life
12%	Opportunities to care for the poor and needy
12%	Regularly meeting with a mentor
12%	My family attending

n=4,964 Christians ages 18 to 35 who attend church at least a few times every six months, December 4, 2018–February 15, 2019. Respondents could select all that apply. For the chart on the right, respondents were not shown options they had selected for the first chart. Only the top 10 responses are shown here.

NEARLY ONE-FIFTH OF CHURCHGOING CHRISTIANS
(18%) SAYS THEIR FRIENDS ARE ABSENT FROM
THEIR CHURCH EXPERIENCE

adults, particularly in secular contexts—but regardless of the religious climate in which these Christians live, friends are still identified as the main thing missing (20% in secular climates, 18% in Christian climate, 14% in multi-faith climates). Relatedly, social gatherings outside of services (14%), relationship workshops (14%) or support groups (13%) are also among the top things lacking from young Christians' church experiences.

Meanwhile, social aspects of church life—such as community involvement (24%), small groups (14%), multigenerational friendship (14%), support groups (13%), gatherings outside of service (12%) or mentors (9%)—aren't commonly selected as reasons for participation. Just 14 percent say they attend because someone in their worship community cares deeply about them. The rare mention of these relational reasons for church engagement is perhaps less of a reflection of the stated priorities of young adults and more of a reflection of the perceived offerings of their church environments. In other words, maybe young Christians don't see community as a primary motivator to be at church because their community doesn't exist there to begin with. After all, half of 18–35-year-old Christians (50%) say people at church are judgmental, perhaps one reason some of them feel they don't connect well (35%) or fit in (23%) with a church community.

A similar trend occurs when it comes to opportunities to fight injustice or oppression. This is low on the list of reasons that Christians already participate in their church community (11%), yet comparatively high on the list of things they would like to see more of (17%, just behind the percentage who say "friends"). Still, about one in five does say their church engagement involves caring for the poor and needy (22%), their community (21%) or the world (19%). (See page 112 to learn more about how 18–35-year-olds feel their church is making a difference in the world.)

Clearly, Christians in this study are thinking seriously about their personal spiritual development—but, as members of a connected generation, they hope their community might be included in and improved by this effort. There appears to be a sense that "church life" is distinct from their social circle or even from the issues and problems facing the world. How can churches create attractive environments where spiritual development is better integrated with the whole of young Christians' lives—where discipleship feels less like self-help and more like a group effort?

Why Resilient Faith Matters

BY DAVID KINNAMAN

with contributions from Aly Hawkins

DAVID KINNAMAN
President at Barna Group
UNITED STATES

WE spend a lot of our time at Barna thinking about and exploring the ways faith is shaped—the positive and negative impact of leaders, the influence of physical places, the meaning of rituals and the stickiness of relationships, among many others. Of course, research has limitations; any good researcher should admit this. Yet social research is better than our best guesses and helps to cut through the clutter of anecdotes.

I have been writing about the next generation for a while now, starting in 2007 with *unChristian* and then in 2011 with *You Lost Me*, trying to help Christian leaders prepare for the Church's future. The data Barna gathered in those studies tell us a lot about what the Christian community, particularly in a U.S. context, was getting wrong when it came to forming young disciples—which is helpful information for making necessary course corrections.

But our team also knew, from conducting over 100,000 interviews with teens and young adults across more than a decade, that churches were getting some things right. But which things? It was time to do more research.

In *Faith for Exiles: 5 Ways for a New Generation to Follow Jesus in Digital Babylon*, my coauthor, Mark Matlock, and I contend that accelerated cultural change prompts us to revive the biblical metaphor of exile as a helpful description of today's Christian experience. We call this place of exile "digital Babylon"—comparative in size and power to the ancient empire that took God's people into captivity, but armed with weapons we willingly use on ourselves: our screens.

Like it or not, screens disciple. Yes, they inform and connect. But they also distract and entertain. Increasingly, they are the grid through which we evaluate what's true or false, what's real or not. Through their ubiquitous presence and our unthinking consumption, the values of Babylon—power, pleasure, prestige—are discipled right into our hearts, minds and souls.

Mark and I identify four groups of exiles, young adults who share a Christian background: **prodigals**, **nomads**, **habitual churchgoers** and **resilient disciples**. In adulthood, they demonstrate marked differences in their beliefs and practices. One in 10 U.S. young adults raised in church is a *resilient disciple*—and by looking at what they have in common, we can observe the kinds of faith-forming environments that are most valuable for passing on vibrant, lasting faith to the next generation.

Because that's the hope, right? That our faith communities would raise children and teens who grow into adults who know, love and follow Jesus, and who steward his Church into an unknown future with courage and wisdom. We believe those who are best equipped to do so are "resilient"—that is, they not only *maintain* faith during adversity but actually *deepen* their confidence in and commitment to Christ through the challenges they face. They are resilient against superficial Christianity, which inoculates so many churchgoing youth to the power of the gospel, and resilient against the faith-corroding enticements of digital Babylon.

My friend Steve, who spent many years in healthcare, reminds me that to understand well-being we have to study the habits of the healthiest people, not just the maladies of the sick. Similarly, Jesus told the parable of the sower to demonstrate that his kingdom grows from good soil. In that spirit, our research among resilient disciples has yielded "soil samples" we can analyze to find out what cultivation factors contribute to their healthy, flourishing discipleship.

Faith for Exiles details what we discovered in the U.S. When it came time to launch the global research for *The Connected Generation,* our team wondered if we would observe similar patterns of Christian faithfulness around the world.

Introducing Exiles

Base: Grew up with some type of Christian background

		ALL	U.S.
✖	**Prodigals**	21%	22%
◉	**Nomads**	37%	30%
⛪	**Habitual churchgoers**	30%	38%
▪	**Resilient disciples**	13%	10%

This data only looks at those who grew up Christian and their current relationship to Christianity; others who did not have Christian experiences before age 18 are not shown in this table or analyzed in this chapter. U.S. percentages are from the *Faith for Exiles* research, conducted in February 2018 among 1,514 U.S. 18–29-year-olds who grew up as Christians. Global / "all" percentages are from this study, conducted December 2018–February 2019, and represent 9,766 18- to 29-year-olds who grew up as Christians.

Prodigals grew up Christian but no longer identify themselves as Christian.

Nomads identify as Christian but do not regularly attend church.

Habitual churchgoers identify as Christian and attend church at least once a month, but do not qualify as resilient disciples.

Resilient disciples identify as Christian and (1) attend a local church regularly and engage with their faith community above and beyond worship services, (2) trust firmly in the authority of the Bible, (3) are committed to Jesus personally and affirm his death and resurrection and (4) express a desire for their faith to impact their words and actions.

In short: yes! Resilient disciples can be found in each of the 25 nations included in this study, and across Christian traditions and denominations.

This generation doesn't just want to know whether Christianity is true; they want to see that it is good. So let's not breeze by this remarkable fact: God has placed, is preparing and is already using resilient young Christians around the world. If you're wondering what God is up to and where the Church may be headed in your nation, talk to a resilient disciple.

THIS GENERATION DOESN'T JUST WANT TO KNOW WHETHER CHRISTIANITY IS TRUE; THEY WANT TO SEE THAT IT IS GOOD

Resilient Faith in the Global Context

In the global study, we discovered that roughly one out of seven 18–35-year-olds (13%) who grew up as a Christian has the marks of a resilient disciple. One-third of connected generation Christians are habitual churchgoers, who are active in a faith community but lack some or all of the marks of resilient faith. The remaining young exiles are either nomads (37%), who still call themselves Christian but have lapsed in faith practice, or prodigals (21%), those for whom the label no longer fits. (There are far too many in these latter two groups. More than half the global audience of young adults with a Christian background report faith in decline. It's

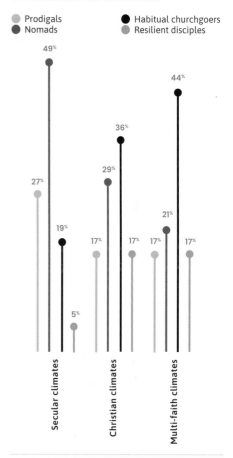

EXILES SEGMENTS, BY RELIGIOUS CLIMATE

● Prodigals   ● Habitual churchgoers
● Nomads   ● Resilient disciples

Secular climates: 49%, 27%, 19%, 5%
Christian climates: 36%, 29%, 17%, 17%
Multi-faith climates: 44%, 21%, 17%, 17%

n=9,766 adults ages 18 to 35 who who grew up with some type of Christian background, December 4, 2018–February 15, 2019.

a holy privilege for us to listen to and respectfully retell the stories of those who de-convert; they are not easy to hear. Even as this chapter focuses on the exemplars of resilience, let's not forget to pray for and reach out to nomads and prodigals.)

Our team found strong quantitative

MORE THAN HALF THE GLOBAL AUDIENCE OF YOUNG ADULTS WITH A CHRISTIAN BACKGROUND REPORT FAITH IN DECLINE

corroboration of anecdotal evidence we've been seeing for years: It is more difficult to be a Christian with resilient faith in a post-Christian or secular climate than in a Christian or even a non-Christian or multi-faith religious climate. As the chart shows, the experience most common to young adults raised Christian in a secular climate is that of the nomads—that is, lapsed faith.

The work of disciple-making is not easy in any context, but barriers are often more easily surmounted in a majority-religious climate. Regular churchgoing and high-priority spiritual life are simpler propositions in a culture that also values religious practice.

These findings are stark evidence that secular climates are hard on resilient faith. Digital Babylon is uniquely unfriendly to exiles who want to follow Christ.

Context matters. If you're in a post-Christian or emerging post–Christian context (such as the U.S.), discipleship faces rough headwinds on the path to resilience. You'll likely have the wind at your back if you're in a majority-religious setting, but there are unique challenges for disciple-

ship in those environments, as well. If you want to make and be a resilient disciple, understand your context.

Defining Discipleship

The point of studying resilient disciples is not to draw theological lines but to help us think through how we define discipleship. People from different cultures or Christian traditions may disagree on the merits of the factors we selected to define this group. You may find them to be either too lenient or too stringent; you might have chosen different qualifiers. That's fine! Even if you don't use *our* metric, you need *a* metric.

How are you defining effective discipleship?

What does resilient faith look like in your context?

One of the things we've learned in more than three decades of research is that you get what you measure. If you only measure warm bodies—a church packed with Millennial and Gen Z attenders—you get spectators to the faith. You get young people who are not prepared to be in-but-not-of the world. You get young adults who say they are Christian but are not wholly transformed by the light of the gospel or the power of the Spirit.

You get nomads, prodigals and habitual churchgoers.

Resilient young disciples, as we define them, don't happen by accident. What are you measuring?

There are times and places where faith is at the center, and times and places where faith is pushed to the margins. In digital Babylon, where information and *things* are instantly available at the godlike swipe of a finger, Almighty God has been squeezed to the margins. This transition—from faith at the center to faith at the margins—is nearly complete in post-Christian climates such as the UK, Canada, Germany and Australia, and fully underway in still majority-Christian United States. In order to make disciples in this newly unfriendly culture, we have to adapt our methods and priorities. With that in mind, *Faith for Exiles* offers the following as the goal (and, therefore, a metric) for discipleship: *to develop Jesus followers who are resiliently faithful in the face of cultural coercion and who live a vibrant life in the Spirit.*

Though we've had tremendous international collaboration and input for this specific research effort, I am conscious of our team's perspective (and limits) as a group primarily made up of American Christians. But I believe this definition of discipleship, even though it's coming from a particular cultural reality that is not shared by everyone, can be helpful to Christian leaders in many different cultures. Let's unpack each of the component parts.

To develop Jesus followers. Our ultimate aim must be to make deep, lasting connections between young people and Jesus, "who initiates and perfects our faith" and endured the cross and its shame to joyfully redeem the world (Hebrews 12:2). Those who follow him also undertake his joyful mission of redemption.

Who are resiliently faithful in the face of cultural coercion. Resilience is a hot topic in business circles, and for good reason; it's what a person, team or company needs in order to emerge from inevitable challenges not only intact but also with refined skills and deeper wisdom. In the realm of faith, resilient disciples grow more like Jesus, not in spite of but *because of* their location in a society that exerts enormous coercive power, as in digital Babylon.

And who live a vibrant life in the Spirit. These Jesus-centered, culture-countering people adopt a way of life that is obviously different from the powerful norms of go-with-the-flow life in the screen age.[25]

Here is the great news: Some of these disciples already exist.

Connection & Resilience

What can we learn from the spiritual lives and inputs of resilient Christians around the world? They are growing into faithful adults and, among the majority, church experiences have something to do with it. Nearly six in 10 say they were "very active" practicing Christianity in their teenage years (56%), compared with 28 percent of other self-identified Christians (nomads and habitual churchgoers). They also tend to strongly agree they had adult, non-family friends in their church when they were growing up (61% vs. 28%), so parents and grandparents weren't their only models of adult faithfulness.

Asked about their current church, resilient disciples and habitual churchgoers—who are, by definition, equally likely to attend worship services—report quite different experiences:

- My church has helped me better understand my purpose in life (78% resilient disciples vs. 55% habitual churchgoers).
- At church, I have learned how the Bible applies to my field or interest area (63% vs. 38%).
- My church has helped me to better live out my faith in the workplace (63% vs. 36%).
- I have been inspired to live generously based on the example of people at my church (57% vs. 35%).
- My church has helped me better understand the needs of the poor (55% vs. 32%).

From this list it's clear that resilient discipleship is much more than what happens in church. It's also about what happens by virtue of faith outside the sanctuary, in the world—in the workplace, in the arena of calling and vocation, in the realm of generosity and money, in serving others. That's one of the clearest demarcations of resilient disciples: Their faith compels them to be much more than dutiful, nice, smiling-emoji churchgoers.

There is ample evidence that their faith is vibrant in other ways, too. For instance, most young resilient disciples strongly agree there is someone in their life who encourages them to grow spiritually (84% vs. 39% other Christians). Regular attendance at worship services is important for *maintaining* faith, but it's not enough to reliably *grow* faith—at least not on its own. For faith to grow, church must be the place where young Christians practice following Jesus *alongside other believers* who help them discover how to bring faith into every area of their lives.

Unsurprisingly, given the consistent expressions of relational and spiritual well-being from resilient

CONNECTIVITY, BY EXILE SEGMENT

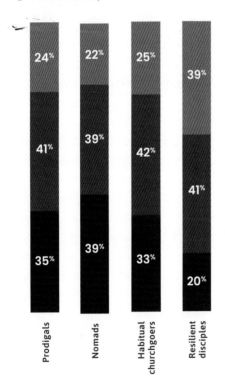

- Strong connectivity
- Medium connectivity
- Weak connectivity

	Prodigals	Nomads	Habitual churchgoers	Resilient disciples
Strong	24%	22%	25%	39%
Medium	41%	39%	42%	41%
Weak	35%	39%	33%	20%

n=9,766 adults ages 18 to 35 who grew up with some type of Christian background, December 4, 2018–February 15, 2019.

disciples, these young Christians are significantly more likely than exiles in the other three groups to score as "strong" on the connectivity index—and much less likely to score as "weak." (For more on this concept, read "From Chaos to Connectivity"

RESILIENT DISCIPLES DISPLAY SOME OF THE HEALTHIEST LEVELS OF CONNECTION OVERALL

on page 20) And though they are just as apt as others to fall in the middle of the index, they tend to score closer to strong than weak. In other words, resilient disciples display some of the healthiest levels of connection overall: They are more globally connected, relationally connected, personally empowered and outwardly oriented than most of their peers. Their faith commitments make a positive, discernible difference in their lives.

Cultivate Resilience

Faith for Exiles proposes five practices that grow resilient faith—of course, it took Mark and me an entire book to unpack them, and I have a word limit for this chapter! But here are four next steps to get you going:

1. **Be encouraged.** God is alive and at work, changing the hearts and lives of millions of 18–35-year-olds around the world. Young resilient Christians *are* to be found in your context. What can you do to learn from them, to invest in them— not just to solve problems, but to journey together and launch them into their God-ordained destiny? Don't simply try to attract and entertain young Christians; engage them in the work. It's not church *for* them. It should be church *with* them.

2. **Understand your context.** Take stock of your surrounding religious climate. What are the forces at work that arrest or accelerate disciple-making where you are? Be ready to adapt your methods and priorities accordingly.

3. **Measure the right stuff.** You get what you measure. How do you measure effective discipleship? What metrics are you using to evaluate the kind of disciples your ministry is cultivating?

4. **Search the scriptures** for inspiration about the kind of resilient people God is calling us to be. Stories of exile are the place to start: Daniel, Esther, Joseph, Jeremiah, 1 Peter— the biblical witness of faithfulness in exile is a reliable guide for resilient faith. ●

COUNTRY COMPARISON

RESILIENCE AROUND THE WORLD

TYPES OF EXILES, BY COUNTRY

● Resilient disciples ● Habitual churchgoers ● Nomads ● Prodigals

AUSTRALIA
● 8%
● 22%
● 35%
● 35%

AUSTRIA
● 1%
● 13%
● 67%
● 19%

BRAZIL
● 17%
● 42%
● 28%
● 13%

CANADA
● 9%
● 22%
● 47%
● 22%

CHILE
● 10%
● 19%
● 43%
● 28%

COLOMBIA
● 13%
● 38%
● 27%
● 23%

GERMANY
● 2%
● 17%
● 55%
● 26%

GHANA
● 34%
● 46%
● 12%
● 7%

INDIA
● 16%
● 53%
● 8%
● 22%

INDONESIA
● 20%
● 64%
● 15%
● 2%

KENYA
● 33%
● 49%
● 14%
● 5%

MALAYSIA
● 24%
● 41%
● 24%
● 10%

MEXICO
● 6%
● 38%
● 36%
● 20%

NEW ZEALAND
● 9%
● 24%
● 33%
● 34%

NIGERIA
● 41%
● 43%
● 7%
● 9%

PHILIPPINES
● 12%
● 54%
● 26%
● 9%

ROMANIA
● 3%
● 29%
● 60%
● 8%

SINGAPORE
● 22%
● 38%
● 21%
● 19%

SOUTH AFRICA
● 20%
● 34%
● 28%
● 18%

SOUTH KOREA
● 9%
● 42%
● 27%
● 22%

SPAIN
● 4%
● 21%
● 52%
● 24%

SWITZERLAND
● 3%
● 13%
● 49%
● 35%

TAIWAN
● 2%
● 33%
● 38%
● 27%

UNITED KINGDOM
● 4%
● 23%
● 49%
● 23%

UNITED STATES
● 10%
● 38%
● 30%
● 22%

n=9,766 adults ages 18 to 35 who grew up with some type of Christian background, December 4, 2018–February 15, 2019.

Connect the Dots:
Engagement with Spirituality
& the Church

REFLECTIONS AND NEXT STEPS
INSPIRED BY THE RESEARCH

See the whole.

- Most teens and young adults sense there's more going on than what they can see with their eyes. They are aware of spiritual realities beyond the material stuff of life, and many express warmth toward spiritual engagement.

- This generation is not only interested in whether Christianity is true; they also want to see that it is good. Hypocrisy, suffering, wars and science are sources of doubt for many young people who might otherwise be drawn to faith. The data show there are Christians across the globe who are living good stories, who have a strong sense of connection with the world and with others around them.

- The overall religious climate of a particular culture matters when it comes to sustaining resilient faith into adulthood. In places where regular religious practice and high-priority spirituality are not the norm, disciples need extra support from their community of faith.

Take time to pray.

- For God to reveal himself to young people who are already sensitive to spiritual realities; for young Christians to sink deep, sustaining roots into the scriptures, their church family and a life of prayer.

- For the particular challenges of your religious climate; for leaders to act with wisdom to end wars and human suffering; for Christians to act and speak with integrity and compassion.

- For your community to live out the way of Christ without hypocrisy; for wisdom to engage well with questions of science.

Create what's next.

- *Listen.* Find out what spiritual experiences young people are already having. What issues or experiences are keeping them from faith?

- *Think.* How are you and your community showing that Christianity is both true and good? What needs to change? How can you partner with other groups and organizations in this good work?

- *Act* with integrity and sincerity. Share—and live—the gospel in ways that make sense culturally and relationally.

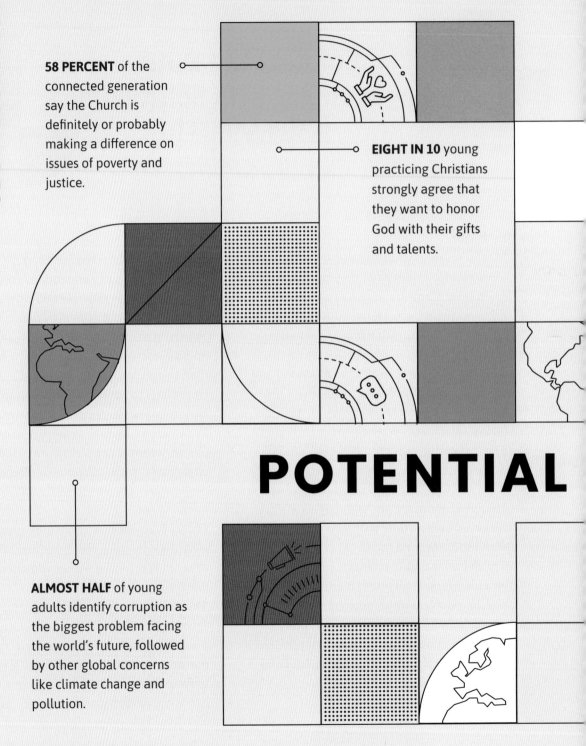

58 PERCENT of the connected generation say the Church is definitely or probably making a difference on issues of poverty and justice.

EIGHT IN 10 young practicing Christians strongly agree that they want to honor God with their gifts and talents.

POTENTIAL

ALMOST HALF of young adults identify corruption as the biggest problem facing the world's future, followed by other global concerns like climate change and pollution.

82 PERCENT of respondents feel there is a crisis of leadership today. Half identify busyness and distraction as a challenge, and 30 percent have never thought of themselves as a leader.

FOR IMPACT

FEATURING

Ruth Yimika Afolabi, Juliette Arulrajah, Abel Cheah, Daniel Flynn, Krish Kandiah, Chine McDonald, Percy Mongwai, Daniel Muvengi, Stephen Proctor, Sifiso Pule, Joy Beth Smith, Wesley Teixeira, Tracy Trinita

Q & A

Stories of Impact

LEADERS WHO REPRESENT OR WORK WITH EMERGING
GENERATIONS SHARE IDEAS ABOUT CALLING, PURPOSE
AND CONNECTION

What does it mean to you to feel a sense of "calling?"

JULIETTE: I believe that calling is an extremely strong conviction motivated by God, which propels a person to move with passion, priority and purpose. Calling is intertwined with one's life purpose and can be expressed differently through a variety of careers at different stages of one's life. For example, if one feels their calling is to help alleviate poverty, this could be expressed by being an educator at first, then going on to work for an NGO, then to business or even politics.

JULIETTE ARULRAJAH
Regional Co-Facilitator for
Transform World Southeast Asia
SINGAPORE

DANIEL: Deep down, we all have a sense of calling. The scriptures definitely confirm it. I just wonder if that gets robbed sometimes by the sense of comparison that so plagues humanity. We compare to the journey of others, maybe even envy the "fingerprint" of someone else, without realizing we have a unique call.

STEPHEN: To me, "calling" is where my passion and purpose intersect. It's that thing I can't help but do or create, even if it's challenging or painful. It's when my desires and skills line up with what the world so desperately needs. It's what lights me up, but it's also what burdens me. Pay attention to what gets you "in the zone," that thing that fires you up so much that you can't fall asleep. If you get paid for it, realize what a rare privilege it is! Your job and calling don't have to be the

ABEL CHEAH
National Coordinator of
Alpha Malaysia
MALAYSIA

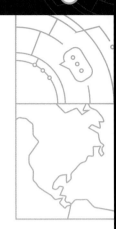

> "YOUR JOB AND CALLING DON'T HAVE TO BE THE SAME THING, SO HAVING THE 'PERFECT DREAM JOB' SHOULD NEVER BE AN EXPECTATION OR AN ENTITLEMENT."

same thing, so having the "perfect dream job" should never be an expectation or an entitlement.

What advice would you give to young adults who are anxious about career decisions?

ABEL: Keep learning and investing in relationships at all levels. A posture of learning enables you to develop two highly important and transferable skills you'll need to thrive in your work: self-awareness and adaptability. Learn to ask questions and develop intellectual and relational curiosity with everyone at all levels, believing that you can learn anything from anyone.

DANIEL: The future is unknown, there are so many possible paths, and everyone expects you to have it figured out. I grew up with my mom and dad quoting the scripture, "Be anxious about nothing."

They quoted it as an encouragement for me to pray about my future. So that's what I did. I didn't have the answer pop up straight away, but there is something remarkable about not internalizing that anxious wrestling about future decisions and to look up (pray) and seek the wisdom of people you trust in your life.

JOY: One of my college professors always said, "Get your foot in the door, and then figure out how to open it." I have followed this advice throughout my career, and it's benefited me in countless ways by providing opportunities I never would have had otherwise. Company culture matters, working with people you like matters, and getting a start in a new field (no matter what role you're playing) matters. So, don't hold out for the dream job—just get your foot in the door. Our career paths will likely look so much different than we imagine.

PERCY: Many young people choose their careers based on the urgency to meet their basic needs. In my experience, careers chosen with this in mind can cause a lot of frustration and lack of fulfillment. It is when one is within their God-given purpose, gift or calling that they can enjoy the fulfilment and satisfaction of their career. The impact to those receiving your time and service is even greater.

TRACY: We need to be agile and open-minded within the corridor of values and principles. Sometimes we need quality people to affirm our talents. Sometimes by helping others wholeheartedly we can unearth the hidden capacity within us. Most importantly, pray to God for divine guidance on what we should do next and where we should be. While waiting in prayer, do something. I love the Bible verse, "Do not despise these small beginnings" (Zechariah 4:10).

"SOMETIMES BY HELPING OTHERS WHOLEHEARTEDLY WE CAN UNEARTH THE HIDDEN CAPACITY WITHIN US."

What are some benefits and what are some drawbacks of the feeling of connectedness the internet provides?

JOY: The internet has offered me solace and hope when I thought I was alone. It has given me access to teachers who have patiently guided me through lessons on racial reconciliation and healthy sexuality. It has provided cheerleaders for my successes and wise counsel for my questions. But the internet has also decreased my desire to plant roots in a new town because I already receive support and engagement online. It has preoccupied me by staving off my need for emotional intimacy and convincing me I'm known, but it never truly satisfies. It has reduced the importance of introspection and mystery as I derive value from the amount I can disclose and the number of engagements I can receive in return. Ultimately, the internet is both wonderful and terrible. Balance in all things is necessary. While the internet offers many

great gifts, it can and should never be a replacement for the embodied life we're called to.

SIFISO: The internet has enabled people to access communities they self-identify with at an exponential scale, and it enables fast dissemination of information in a decentralized manner. This is both a good thing and a bad thing in that it has enabled those same individuals and communities to become polarized, leading to fragmentation and forced assimilation: "You're either with us or you're against us." The internet has been elevated as the primary source of "truth," which has led to mass deception and mass social engineering to conform to particular interest groups' set of norms.

How do you think the internet and social media has impacted the work of social justice?

DANIEL: Before social media, many dark areas of society were known about, but not seen. Now we have light shining on local and global issues like never before. We have calls to action. This is awesome, and also overwhelming. "Charity fatigue," or the feeling that there are so many dark prob-

DANIEL FLYNN
Founder of Thankyou Water
AUSTRALIA

PERCY MONGWAI
Pastor at Hope Restoration Ministry
SOUTH AFRICA

STEPHEN PROCTOR
Visual artist
UNITED STATES

lems in the world, can make people feel paralyzed to step out and create change.

JULIETTE: The reach, connectivity, power and speed of the media have been great assets in creating awareness, mobilizing a variety of helps, harnessing the wider community's resources, researching matters and bringing about a positive outcome or solution for a cause. On the other hand, social media has been used by individuals and groups to abuse the vulnerability of the disadvantaged and generate income for themselves, with little or none of the monies collected being used for the stated purpose of helping the poor or marginalized. Social media, a boon to lifestyles in so many ways, needs to be stewarded wisely and with integrity to maximize its potential for the good of humankind.

ABEL: It has been commonly said that the internet can produce "armchair warriors," people who take a backseat in terms of social justice and are only making online noise. I only agree with this sentiment partially, because while it is true that the anonymity of the internet can create more passive commenters, this is not necessarily unique to Millennials. I believe there is a net benefit to the internet and the growth of social justice movements, and this can be seen in the way societies connected to the internet are becoming more informed, more equal and more connected.

Do you find 18–35-year-olds' openness to spirituality surprising?

STEPHEN: I don't find this surprising at all. My fellow pilgrims and I have been on a journey for the last few years, returning to a more ancient, sacramental expression of faith that is rooted in history and in sync with the global Church. We are weary of churches defined by marketing gimmicks, branding and high production value; we desire a slower sacred space where we can commune, read scripture, be il-luminated by beauty and lament injustice (in political but not partisan ways). It's slow, and it's not entertaining. But it breathes life back into our cynical souls. As my priest says, "Stillness will become our salvation."

ABEL: The Millennial generation is the generation that is most connected and exposed to new and different ideas and cultures. Because choice is important to Millennials, new ideas and bodies of knowledge are more readily accepted. A non-Christian Millennial might be more open to exploring Christianity; however, they might struggle with the notion of choosing Christ alone as the only way to truth. Millennials are generally skeptical of monopolies of thought and ideas, potentially seeing this as a form of inequity.

What do you think young adults are craving from local churches?

TRACY: I asked a youth worker at a church in the UK what she sees as the three most common problems found among the Christian students at Oxford University. Her answer: "First, depression. Second, loneliness. And third, a yearning about their calling in life." Millennials want to know how biblical texts apply to these problems, which are echoed throughout the world, along with questions of identity, sexuality, wealth and possessions, suffering, meaning in life, the purpose of our existence.

PERCY: I feel the Church should have more of a voice on things that are trending in current culture. More often than not, we tend to be more reactive than proactive toward what's going on in culture. We should have more debates and talks inside and outside the Sunday experience to address such topics, especially those that are not necessarily black and white in the Bible.

SIFISO PULE
Township Reformation
SOUTH AFRICA

JOY BETH SMITH
Author, branded content strategy
for *Christianity Today*
UNITED STATES

TRACY TRINITA
Speaker & apologist for Ravi Zacharias
International Ministries (RZIM)
INDONESIA

"IF CHURCHES CLAIM TO VALUE THE PRESENCE OF YOUNG PEOPLE BUT THEY HAVE NO MILLENNIALS IN LEADERSHIP, THAT CHURCH IS NOT TRULY COMMITTED TO YOUNG PEOPLE."

JULIETTE: Church leaders could better address young adults' needs, concerns and questions by intentionally seeking them out to form genuine, caring relationships where deep conversations and dialogue can occur. This would be like a nursery or seedbed for growing understanding between the two groups and minimizing the communication / generation gap.

SIFISO: Young people across all generations have been and are still looking for answers to life's hardest questions. Church leaders must be unashamed and unapologetic about teaching and holding to the authority of God's Word as a single source of truth. God's Word is sufficient for addressing all aspects of life even in our postmodern and increasingly polarized digital age. Churches need to leverage the benefits of technology to enable Millennials to find answers to their questions across all subjects and channels.

JOY: If churches claim to value the presence and contributions of young people but they have no Millennials in leadership positions, no Millennials under mentorship and no Millennials being asked to join decision-making committees, then that church is not truly committed to young people. You can always tell what a church (or person) supports based on its budget and calendar. Until those calendars and budgets more closely reflect average Millennials—who are more likely to be racially diverse and overwhelmed with debt and less likely to be married or own their own home—then the church will continue to lose these vital members. ●

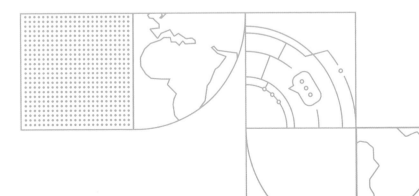

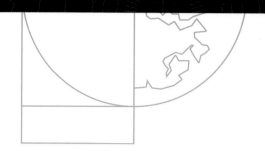

More Than Words

HOW THE CHURCH IS ENGAGING A GENERATION WITH A LONGING FOR JUSTICE

According to many Christians in this study, caring for the poor and vulnerable is a defining characteristic of being a Christ-follower (43%). If this is a primary sign that someone is a Christian, what kind of impression are faithful 18–35-year-olds leaving around the world?

Overall, *a slight majority of respondents feels the Church is definitely (16%) or probably (42%) making a difference on issues of poverty and justice.* Christians and those who identify with no faith, however, differ considerably on how successful the work of the Church has been. Nearly three-quarters of Christians think the Church is making a difference (73% "definitely" + "probably"), compared to only a third of those who claim no faith (32% "definitely" + "probably"). Members of other faiths are essentially split down the middle (55% "definitely" + "probably"). This difference in opinion could be taken as a direct reflection of the Church's actions (or inaction) or evidence of varying interpretations or benchmarks of what it means to work for justice.

In their personal lives, at least, Christian young adults say their beliefs inspire them toward action. More than half (56%) say they are concerned about the welfare of others because of their beliefs. They are also almost twice as likely as those with no faith to be inspired to give of their time to help others in need (56% to 32%). Similarly, Christian young adults are more likely than those with no faith to report that their beliefs compel them to give of their own resources (46% to 26%) and stand up against corruption (47% to 37%). Though these values set Christian 18–35-year-olds apart from those who don't belong to a religion, they are similar to the responses of members of other faith groups when asked how their priorities are affected by their belief system.

While it's clear that religious young adults believe it is important to give their time and resources to help others, there is a stark difference when comparing the actual behaviors of those who practice their faith—that is, religious respondents who say their faith is important and regularly attend worship services—and those who are non-practicing. For instance, practicing Christians are twice as likely as non-practicing Christians to say they volunteer at least once a month (39% to 16%). When it comes to donations, they are more inclined to give money to a local charity at least one a month (23% vs. 13%), and three times more likely to report giving money specifically to a Christian charity at the same frequency (27% vs. 9%). Half of prac-

HOW THE CHURCH ENCOURAGES COMPASSION & ACTIVISM

"Which of the following, if any, have you experienced in your church, parish or faith community?"

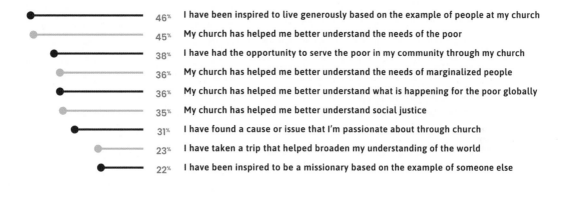

46% I have been inspired to live generously based on the example of people at my church

45% My church has helped me better understand the needs of the poor

38% I have had the opportunity to serve the poor in my community through my church

36% My church has helped me better understand the needs of marginalized people

36% My church has helped me better understand what is happening for the poor globally

35% My church has helped me better understand social justice

31% I have found a cause or issue that I'm passionate about through church

23% I have taken a trip that helped broaden my understanding of the world

22% I have been inspired to be a missionary based on the example of someone else

n=2,896 practicing Christian adults ages 18 to 35, December 4, 2018–February 15, 2019.

ticing Christians (50%) also give to their place of worship each month (vs. 14%), which may also be seen as an opportunity to support mission or justice initiatives.

When the scope of activity is widened—from the past month to the past three years—many of these differences remain, underscoring the consistency of young practicing Christians. Over this span of time, some practicing Christians have taken additional steps such as sponsoring a child (17%) or living or traveling internationally to volunteer (11%). Though practicing Christians are eager to report generally having raised awareness for meaningful causes (28%), non-practicing

Christians, or even members of no faith, are more likely to have taken specific action by signing petitions (38% and 45%, respectively, compared to 27% for practicing Christians), which could be a reflection of either their preferred methods of activism or the scale of the problems they prioritize.

How does faith factor into the causes 18–35-year-olds care about? ***Young adults who aren't religious are far more likely to identify global climate change as the greatest problem facing the world's future*** (46%), but the closer respondents are to religion, the less likely they are to share this environmental concern (27% of practicing Christians, 26% of those practicing other faiths). Instead, corruption—perhaps because it is perceived as a moral problem—tops the list of pressing

TOP FIVE GLOBAL PROBLEMS

TOTAL

44%	37%	35%	32%	32%
Corruption	Global climate change	Pollution	Racism	Extreme poverty

PRACTICING CHRISTIANS

54%	35%	33%	29%	27%
Corruption	Extreme poverty	Racism	Pollution	Hunger and famines

NO FAITH

46%	39%	37%	31%	29%
Global climate change	Pollution	Corruption	Extreme poverty	Racism

n=15,369 adults ages 18 to 35, December 4, 2018–February 15, 2019.

YOUNG ADULTS WHO AREN'T RELIGIOUS ARE FAR MORE LIKELY TO IDENTIFY GLOBAL CLIMATE CHANGE AS THE GREATEST PROBLEM FACING THE WORLD'S FUTURE

one in four young adults says caring for the poor is one of their goals for the next 10 years, and opportunities to fight injustice is among the top things religious respondents say they want more of in their worship community. Even so, Christians who engage meaningfully with their faith and church tend to report that their church has already helped them understand the needs of the poor (45%) and marginalized (36%) and provided opportunities to serve those in need in their community (38%). Similarly, about *a third of practicing Christians says their church has equipped them with an understanding of social justice* (35%) or that they've found a cause or issue they're passionate about through their church (31%).

There is a clear connection between faith practice and social action. Churches have the unique opportunity to provide room for members of this connected generation to learn more about, become engaged with and maybe even change the world. ●

global problems identified by practicing members of Christianity (54%) as well as other faiths (55%, compared to 37% of no faith). Beyond that, practicing Christians are like their peers in ranking extreme poverty (35%) and racism (33%) among key threats to the world's future.

Though the methods and motivations may vary, the data show a pervasive sense of humanitarian responsibility across many segments in this study, and the Church can foster these passions. After all,

COUNTRY COMPARISON

TOP GLOBAL CONCERNS

What do you believe is the greatest problem facing the world's future? Respondents were asked to select, from a list of potential issues, which issues worry them most. A clear top five emerged, some global in nature: corruption, climate change, pollution, racism and extreme poverty. Below, we'll look at the most common concerns identified by the plurality of 18–35-year-olds from each nation included in the survey.

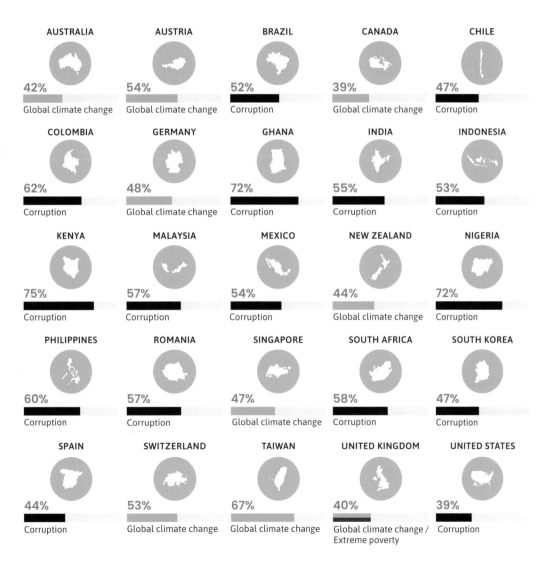

AUSTRALIA	AUSTRIA	BRAZIL	CANADA	CHILE
42%	54%	52%	39%	47%
Global climate change	Global climate change	Corruption	Global climate change	Corruption

COLOMBIA	GERMANY	GHANA	INDIA	INDONESIA
62%	48%	72%	55%	53%
Corruption	Global climate change	Corruption	Corruption	Corruption

KENYA	MALAYSIA	MEXICO	NEW ZEALAND	NIGERIA
75%	57%	54%	44%	72%
Corruption	Corruption	Corruption	Global climate change	Corruption

PHILIPPINES	ROMANIA	SINGAPORE	SOUTH AFRICA	SOUTH KOREA
60%	57%	47%	58%	47%
Corruption	Corruption	Global climate change	Corruption	Corruption

SPAIN	SWITZERLAND	TAIWAN	UNITED KINGDOM	UNITED STATES
44%	53%	67%	40%	39%
Corruption	Global climate change	Global climate change	Global climate change / Extreme poverty	Corruption

n=15,369 adults ages 18 to 35, December 4, 2018–February 15, 2019.

Q & A

Lifting Children out of Poverty

Our research and others' consistently highlight links between well-being and education. Beyond being more learned, what are some of the benefits of education that you see, particularly for children who grow up in poverty?

For a person whose identity has been marred due to the hard experiences brought about by living in poverty, education brings huge benefits. Education—and, I believe, especially religious education—has a way of opening a person's heart, mind and eyes. Children open their eyes to see the world of possibilities. As they get jobs and opportunities, they tend to move from being isolated to being brought into the center of life decisions. Education gives them a sense of identity, helps them build a vision and lead their own lives positively. Educating the poor for life means expanding their options in life. However, not all poor people who get access to education end up being helpful in society. Education without good values tends to produce greedy people whose agenda is to acquire more at the expense of the poor. Faith provides the right grounding in producing a generation with values and respect for each other.

When asked what they believe are the greatest problems facing the world's future, "extreme poverty" consistently was mentioned in the top five. Christians especially see global poverty as a primary issue. How do you think faith factors into helping solve the issue of poverty?

In many communities that we serve, we equip churches through Empowered World View, a faith-based approach that addresses not only material poverty, but also the poverty of heart, mindsets and relationships. It reaches deep into people's core beliefs, transforming their view of the world so that the cycle of chronic poverty and hopelessness can be broken. It helps people find value in their own identity, create a vision for their future and nurture family and community relationships while demonstrating compassion. A richer understanding of their faith changes how they see the world and their ability to have an influence on their own circumstances. With this approach, we move beyond merely meeting physical needs to accompany individuals on journeys of transformation. ●

DANIEL MUVENGI
Regional director for World Vision
International
KENYA

Q & A

Welcoming the Stranger

Even though we're so digitally connected, people express a lot of difficulty in interpersonal relationships and in finding friends. How can Christian hospitality help in this cultural moment?

Time after time in the Old Testament, we're told that we demonstrate our love for God by how we treat the widow, the orphan and the stranger (or the refugee, as some translations put it). If these are the people who are on God's heart, then surely these people are to be important to us too.

Hospitality calls us to welcome the stranger, not just into our social media groupings, but into our lives and into our homes.

Think about the low moment in the New Testament when the two disciples were walking home from Jerusalem, thinking that the end had come because Jesus had been murdered on a cross by the Roman Imperial power. A stranger comes alongside them and starts to talk to them about Jesus and who he was and what he accomplished. When they get to their homes, the disciples beg the stranger to come inside. It's only when they share bread with him that their eyes are opened, and they see Jesus.

As we welcome the stranger, we welcome Jesus. As we welcome into our hearts and homes the people who are radically different from us or who don't fit the kind of social, economic ethnography that we're used to, that's when we begin to demonstrate something of the grace of God. As we do that, we meet Jesus in the stranger.

What can hospitality look like for young adults who don't feel they have the means to open their home or share their resources?

When the Prophet Elijah was in need, he went to stay with a widow of Zarephath, who had absolutely nothing and shared her last morsel of food with him. Generosity is demonstrated in scripture not by those who are wealthy and give out of their abundance, but by those who share what little they do have.

Hospitality is a frame of mind; it's a posture toward the world. You don't need to own a big house or have a large family to extend hospitality. It can be choosing where you sit in the cafeteria at the school or college or in the workplace. It can be crossing a room to meet someone who feels estranged or socially outcast. For an introvert, offering hospitality can mean going deeper and being faithful to someone who is really wrestling with something. It's having eyes open within your circle of influence to show genuine compassion. ●

KRISH KANDIAH
Founder of Home for Good
UNITED KINGDOM

Q & A

Fighting Injustice

Young adults are sometimes referred to as "slacktivists" because of their generation's reputation for posting about causes on social media but perhaps not getting personally or actively involved. Have you found this to be true?

CHINE: As a Millennial myself, I understand the temptation to "virtue signal"—to signpost our outrage at perceived wrongdoings by certain groups. Potentially it feeds a need associated with social media to make ourselves look good—not just physically beautiful, but morally good. However, my experience of the Millennials I know is that they are some of the most passionate campaigners for justice and equality. They are not satisfied with the wrong in the world and do not feel the need to be silent about their dissatisfaction. This increasingly vocal generation has been signing petitions, marching in protest and volunteering their time for causes. Despite the criticism of "slacktivism," Millennials, generally speaking, are people of community, whether online or offline. Therefore, if people they know, respect and love inspire them to take action in causes that resonate with them, then they are likely to want to get involved.

WESLEY: The majority of the population does not get involved with social causes. In past years, they would talk about it; now, they post about it on social media. I don't think this is something exclusive to the Millennial generation. In Brazil, it has to do with factors such as the long work hours of an impoverished population fighting for subsistence, as well as forms of political control and engrained authoritarianism in our society.

In your experience, what does it take to move these young adults from support on social media to personal involvement?

WESLEY: First of all, social media can help raise awareness of what concrete and assertive law changes, such as bus fare reduction, or preventing school closure or even the unnecessary change of a law others are fighting for. After that, create a proposal for action that can be taken in your own community with your friends and on your free time—something that will not conflict with your work hours and can have a simple communication system. Creating a symbol can help bring the fight from the virtual to the real world. The ease of propagating ideas and creating connections can be used in great ways. Some examples in Brazil are the rallies of June 2013, school occupations, Fighting Harassment at Schools campaign, the Rise of Women and the World Rally Against Climate Change.

One thing young adults say is "missing" from their local church is an opportunity to fight injustice and oppression. Does this ring true in your experience of Christian young adults?

CHINE: This definitely rings true for me. The Christian faith paints a radical picture of how God intended the world to be. Salvation is not just about life after death and it is not solely for the individual. God's big story is about the complete restoration of the whole of creation and reconciliation with God through Christ's incarnation, death and resurrection. So when Millennials who believe in this truth attend churches where the focus is parochial, small and individualistic, when it is dominated by judgment rather than love, when church leaders speak of who's in or out rather than speak out against the injustice and oppression of people made in the image of God, then they walk away.

WESLEY: Nowadays, the theological content offered to youth is very restricted and usually focused on sexual behavior, with a strong appeal to a spirituality disconnected from an interpretation of social reality. We need to begin connecting Bible reading with life in society, and then understand the world and what it means to be young—what the dilemmas are that youth face. We need to engage young people on their day-to-day struggles and fights.

What ways do you think churches can get more involved in these areas? In your experience, is it more effective for churches to partner with existing organizations or to begin / run their own programs?

CHINE: Churches should look first to the needs of the communities in which they find themselves, and then to the national and global issues they might get involved in. There are, of course, many professional Christian and non-Christian organizations that have spent years building up expertise so that they are more effective in bringing about the change they want to see. Many of these organizations are only able to

be effective because of the support of churches and individual Christians. I believe that the problems we are trying to tackle are so great that they can only be tackled by working together. ●

CHINE MCDONALD
Media & PR at Christian Aid; formerly of World Vision UK and the Evangelical Alliance; board member for charities including Greenbelt Festival, the Church & Media Network, Christians Against Poverty and the Sophia Network
UNITED KINGDOM

WESLEY TEIXEIRA
Activist, leader in various movements and demonstrations for favelas and youth of Rio de Janeiro
BRAZIL

Christians Seek Vocational Guidance

HOW ARE CHURCHES HELPING THE 81% OF
PRACTICING CHRISTIANS WHO WANT TO
HONOR GOD WITH THEIR TALENTS?

Few topics have inspired as much handwringing in recent years as the entrance and establishment of Millennials in the workplace. Members of the generation seem perplexed themselves: An international 2019 study from Deloitte found that seven in 10 Millennials don't feel they have all of the skills needed to navigate the future of the job market.[26]

In many ways, career has, thus far into adulthood, been central to 18–35-year-olds' experiences, identity and well-being (see page 37). The majority of respondents in this study (which, bear in mind, is a more educated, resourced sample than would be truly globally representative) is working in some capacity, and for the most part, indicates they are progressing on their personal path of education or career. Whatever their economic uncertainties, many still express hopes of starting businesses, following dreams and living (and purchasing) with financial security in the next decade. But what about something more profound than earning a paycheck or navigating career decisions: a sense of vocation? How is this generation thinking about making an impact? And are churches and spiritual leaders pointing them toward meaningful answers to these questions?

At least among Christian respondents—particularly practicing Christians, those who value their

VOCATIONAL DISCIPLESHIP OPPORTUNITIES

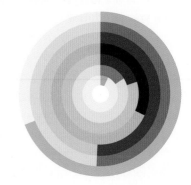

69% My church has helped me better understand my purpose in life

51% At church, I have learned how the Bible applies to my field or interest area

51% My church has helped me to better live out my faith in the workplace

32% I became friends with someone at church who has helped guide my professional development

20% I have access to leadership training for my job through my church

16% Vocational training is missing from my community of worship

7% I participate in my community of worship because of vocational training

n=2,896 practicing Christian adults ages 18 to 35,
December 4, 2018–February 15, 2019.

faith and regularly attend church—there is a desire to use their skills for a distinct purpose. *Eight in 10 young adults who are practicing Christians (81%) say they strongly agree that they want to honor God with their gifts and talents,* compared to just over one-quarter of respondents who are not active Christians (26%).

Church leaders should be heartened that some of their most committed young attendees feel this responsibility or calling—and should be reminded to address this subject directly, practically and consistently. If ministers do, it seems to be effective. If ministers don't, their congregants wish they would; many practicing Christians in this study say they participate in a community of worship in order to learn how to connect their faith to their everyday reality. About half of 18–35-year-old practicing Christians attend services for teachings that are relevant to their lives (49%) and for wisdom to apply scriptures to their lives (46%). Specific to work and career, seven in 10 (69%) say their faith community has helped them understand their purpose in life, and *half say their church has taught them how the Bible applies to their professional field (51%) or how to live out their faith in the workplace (51%).*

Beyond general teaching and sermons, which are common to any ministry and appear to be effective when touching on vocation, some churches may want to increase support of this generation with more intentional, structured opportunities to grow in their skills or callings. Training that is specifically for vocation or leadership isn't particularly high on the list of reasons Christians already participate in a church; it is, however, among the top things Christians in this age group say is missing from their church experience. This is true regardless of a respondent's current employment status or level of education. Vocational training may not rank highly as a present motivation for engagement not because 18–35-year-olds don't want it but because it's rarely offered. Similarly, the proportion of practicing Christians who participates in a church to meet with a mentor is equal to the proportion who says mentorship is absent from their church life (12% each). Even so, one-third of practicing Christian respondents has made a church friend who has helped guide their professional development, suggesting attendees may still naturally find what isn't formally provided or afforded in their community of worship.

For 18–35-year-olds, Christian and non-Christian alike, the future of work and the workplace is fraught. *This connected generation's ambitions are perhaps only matched by their anxieties:* economic woes, threats to work-life balance, pressure from elders, skepticism of employers, fears of waning passion (the latter of which, Barna and other researchers find, is a primary professional motivation for Millennials).[27] Yet faith-filled members of this generation are committed to using their talents to honor God. In large numbers, practicing Christians are relying on their church communities for help in making connections between their religion and their resume, and are attending church to see how the Bible speaks to their purpose and gifts. Yes, next career steps raise worries and questions in Millennials, but Christian communities have a chance to help their members navigate this tricky journey with faith and hope intact. ●

Q & A

Faith & Work

What role have mentors played in your life?

I have about five mentors in my life and, outside of my husband, they've changed my life the most. When I was younger, like 8 or 9 years old, if I was at a friend's house and their parents did something interesting, I would sit down and ask them a million questions about life, about their work, about what it meant to be a parent. I think that led naturally to having a lot of mentors in my life. As I got older, if I found out that a person was doing something related to what I was doing, I'd email them and say, "I know you're super busy, but if you have 15 minutes of time …" Through that, I've built relationships that I've had for [about a decade].

I signed my first modeling contract when I was 19, and I was in a lot of leadership meetings where everyone was a lot older than me. I always thought, "I don't want to get into places and not have anything to say." You always feel like you know everything, but I realized if I could sit down with a mentor and talk to them for two hours, I'd probably save myself five or 10 years.

What advice would you offer to young adults who are starting their careers?

First, wherever you are, you are ultimately working for God. In one of my early jobs, I felt like I wasn't doing God's work. I didn't work for the Church or for a charity. What I learned, though, is that wherever I am, I'm still working for God.

Second, wherever God has placed you in this season, that is a mission field. Around 5 percent of the UK population goes to church regularly.[28] Which means that 95 percent of people at work or in our local communities are probably not going to walk into church anytime soon. If we can shift our focus and have a slightly different perspective—whether we work in a grocery store, in fashion, in a corporate world or even in a local church—we'll see there's so much opportunity wherever God has placed us.

In terms of bringing faith into work, one of my mentors reminded me recently that when someone employs you, they're employing you to do a really good job. In doing a good job, not only are you honoring God, but you are given more opportunity to be a light and an influence. ●

RUTH YIMIKA AFOLABI
Founder of *Magnify* magazine
UNITED KINGDOM

THE PRIMARY OBSTACLE TO LEADERSHIP

What are the biggest challenges to leadership in society today? Most of the 18-35-year-olds Barna surveyed around the world—on average, half (50%)—believe that "everyone is too busy and distracted." In 16 of the 25 nations included in the study, this is the top response selected. Outliers to this trend tend to be more concerned about elder leaders not passing the baton to future generations or about the pressures of vying to succeed in today's economy. Nations where the plurality has other societal obstacles in mind include those where most believe "Older adults are not letting young leaders lead" (Nigeria 70%, Kenya 63%, South Africa 59%, Ghana 58%) and those where more are concerned that "Everyone has to compete now in a global marketplace" (Malaysia 53%, Taiwan 52%, Mexico 50%, Indonesia 45%, Spain 41%).

"THE BIGGEST CHALLENGE TO LEADERSHIP TODAY IS: *EVERYONE IS TOO BUSY AND DISTRACTED*"

Country	%
AUSTRALIA	52%
AUSTRIA	49%
BRAZIL	52%
CANADA	56%
CHILE	59%
COLOMBIA	51%
GERMANY	51%
GHANA	46%
INDIA	60%
INDONESIA	43%
KENYA	47%
MALAYSIA	48%
MEXICO	45%
NEW ZEALAND	51%
NIGERIA	43%
PHILIPPINES	58%
ROMANIA	68%
SINGAPORE	52%
SOUTH AFRICA	57%
SOUTH KOREA	44%
SPAIN	35%
SWITZERLAND	44%
TAIWAN	30%
UNITED KINGDOM	47%
UNITED STATES	55%

n=15,369 adults ages 18 to 35, December 4, 2018–February 15, 2019.

DAVID KINNAMAN
President at Barna Group
UNITED STATES

Developing Connected Leaders

BY DAVID KINNAMAN
with contributions from Aly Hawkins and Alyce Youngblood

S haring a meal together recently, an older successful leader told me, "I would not want to be a young leader starting out today. Everything's just so much more complex, with technology and social media. You have to do all your failing and learning in public." His sentiment echoes our findings: The connected generation faces some unique headwinds on their road to becoming effective leaders.

Part of it is the underlying sense of anxiety that permeates many societies today. For good reason, the connected generation perceives deep, wide, systemic problems facing the world's future. Many of us share their concerns, but most young adults express an added layer of angst: Four out of five affirm—and ***nearly half strongly affirm—that "society is facing a crisis of leadership because there are not enough good leaders right now"*** (82%). This is one of the most widely endorsed statements in the entire global survey, which suggests its significance to this generation. In addition, one-third believes that "what it takes to be an effective leader seems to be changing." Asked about the biggest challenges to good leadership, they express a range of perceptions—from issues of technology, social media and competitive market dynamics, to generational tension in the workplace and the psychology of leading and following:

- Everyone is too busy and distracted (50%).
- Everyone has to compete in a global marketplace (43%).
- Society is becoming so fragmented (41%).
- Older adults are not letting younger leaders actually lead (38%; leaders outside the home are most likely to agree, 43%).
- Younger adults do not want to put in the time to become great leaders (35%; leaders outside the home are most likely to agree, 43%).
- People follow the news headlines instead of leaders (32%).
- No one wants to be a follower anymore (26%).

When we take time to listen—an essential practice for connecting with 18–35-year-olds—we hear a sense of unease about the future and uncertainty about the kind of leaders that could make a difference: *We've got big problems to solve ... who can we trust to lead us?*

Spheres of Leadership

Barna asked young adults in what areas of their life they exercise some level of leadership. Nearly half say they are a leader in their family, and one-third feels like a leader in their workplace or elsewhere, such as a church or government. We group the latter into a category called "leaders outside the home," who are half of all respondents (51%); one in five is a "family-only leader" (19%), meaning they select family as their only sphere of leadership.

Three in 10 young adults do not now (8%) or have never (22%) considered themselves to be a leader; we call them "non-leaders," since that's what they call themselves. Given that male leadership has been the rule of thumb for most of human history, more young women (35%) than young men (26%) are non-leaders. (Relatedly, 57 percent of family-only leaders are women, and women are more likely than men to see gender inequality as a challenge to leadership, 35% vs. 24%.) Since many cultures look first to older members of the community for leadership, those under the age of 25 are more apt than those on the older end of the age range to say they are not leadership material (35% vs. 28%). Unmarried adults, rural residents, those who are less educated and people who report economic insecurity are more likely to reject the "leader" label, compared to married, highly educated, financially stable entrepreneurs who live in the city.

There's a high concentration of young adults in secular climates who do not consider themselves to be leaders (39% vs. 23% Christian climates, 36% multi-faith climates). Every European country in the study has a higher percentage of self-identified non-leaders than the global average. Concurrently, 41 percent of agnostics, atheists and "nones" deny they are a leader in any sphere.

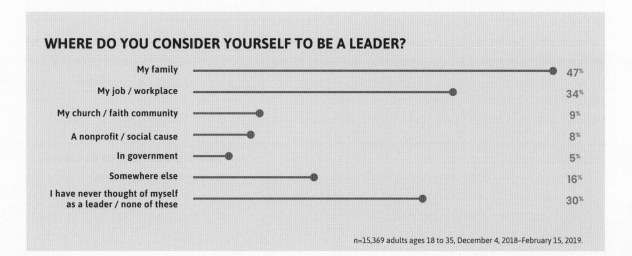

WHERE DO YOU CONSIDER YOURSELF TO BE A LEADER?

My family	47%
My job / workplace	34%
My church / faith community	9%
A nonprofit / social cause	8%
In government	5%
Somewhere else	16%
I have never thought of myself as a leader / none of these	30%

n=15,369 adults ages 18 to 35, December 4, 2018–February 15, 2019.

A Context of Reinvention & Mistrust

Interconnectedness, powered by technology, is transforming how leaders mobilize followers toward a shared goal and how followers perceive their place in the world. It's disruptive—but for many, it's also exciting. If you hang out with young adults in tech hubs like San Francisco, Amsterdam, Nairobi or Singapore, among others cities, it's hard not to catch their enthusiasm to remake the world through connectivity. It's an era of radical reinvention and (mostly) sweeping transparency, and the usual boundaries and borders seem to be shrinking, encroaching on the status quo—with mixed results.

We live in a time of *disintermediation*, a hundred-dollar word that simply describes how the essential connections we've come to rely on to mediate our relationships with other people, organizations, institutions, governments and systems are changing, being redefined or breaking altogether. Amazon, one of the world's largest companies, is a good example of the unbundling, the disintermediation, of the value chain between products and people. Something similar is happening in all sorts of places and industries: in education, in media, in the marketplace, in religion. The connected generation benefits from un- and re-bundling, but often also suffers increased anxiety, mistrust and social dislocation as the institutions that mediate meaning undergo realignment.

Barna data has shown again and again that U.S. Millennials are less likely than older Americans to trust government, social, religious and academic institutions. Now we see a similar tendency in the global findings from 15,000+ surveys. The connected generation is smart, informed, skeptical—and many think they know better. (Sadly, they are sometimes right.)

Their skepticism often extends to faith and religion, too. While many in the connected generation express warmth toward the pastor, priest or faith leader whom they know personally, they are much less likely to extend that warmth to the Church as an institution. Part of this is human nature; affinity correlates with relational proximity. But it's also true that two out of three young adults agree that "there is corruption in the church." Young Christians face high levels of peer skepticism toward the Church—especially but not exclusively in post-Christian climates. Older Christian leaders, at least many with whom I interact in the U.S., don't seem to appreciate just how toxic these perceptions are and how difficult they make it to lead mistrustful teens and adults toward faith.

This is a brief summary of the connected generation's context for leadership. It's a chaotic, reactive, disruptive, anxiety-inducing, rules-are-changing environment characterized by rampant mistrust and deep skepticism. And here we stand, waiting for them to take up the reins and lead.

My older friend was onto something: Would *you* want to lead?

Two Big Challenges to Developing Young Leaders

Good leaders are needed in every culture, and I believe cultivating and then releasing the next generation of resilient Christian leaders is urgent everywhere. Some leadership qualities and principles are timeless and rise above cultural or generational differences: honesty, integrity, conviction and courage, to name a few. But other ideas about what makes a good leader are contextual and therefore not always applicable everywhere to everyone. Problems with and barri-

ers to leadership often differ, as well. *"Leadership" is a concept highly shaped by culture and, increasingly, by generation.* For instance, some societies (and generations) value leaders who exhibit individual merit, personal ambition and orientation toward the future; others esteem leaders who prioritize continuity with the past and handing traditions

and ways of life down from elder to younger members.

This relates to our first challenge to developing young leaders today: Generations perceive and practice leadership differently. Remember, many in the connected generation agree that "what it takes to be an effective leader seems to be changing." Almost every week, I hear from younger leaders and from older, established leaders who are flummoxed by the "the other side" of the generational continuum. Each wants to find a way to work together more effectively but both are thwarted by their differences. A pastor in London said that one of his most urgent issues is figuring how to help young leaders stop being so entitled. And recently a young leader told me she's so exasperated by the authoritarian approach of her supervisor that she's all but ready to leave the organization.

One issue may be language. I've noticed, anecdotally, that many young leaders seem reluctant to actually call themselves "leaders." They want to collaborate. They want "us" to work together, not necessarily with someone out in front. I hear them talk about doing, creating, starting, building, influencing—but less so about leading. Insofar as their reluctance to lead is a result of an eagerness to cooperate, to experiment, to enjoy the collaborative process and to share credit, great! That's leadership—even if you don't call it that. But where their hesitation is rooted in fear, we must call young leaders to be courageous, to take risks. Whether they're feeling overexposed by social media, paralyzed by choice, constrained by those in power or bifurcated when it comes to their inner self and outer persona, young leaders' potential justifications for hanging back are many and, very often, understandable.

THE CONNECTED GENERATION DOESN'T WANT TO BE MERE CONSUMERS; THEY WANT TO BE CONTRIBUTORS

Yet God's calling on leaders from among each generation remains.

If you are trying to develop young leaders, *listen.* What words do they use when they talk about accomplishing great things? When they dream aloud about participating in God's mission? When they brainstorm about starting something new or rewarding?

IF WE'RE NOT MAKING ROOM FOR YOUNGER LEADERS TODAY, THEY WON'T BE AROUND TOMORROW

Speaking of starting new things: Many of them want to. The connected generation doesn't want to be mere consumers; they want to be contributors. Remember the resilient disciples we met on page 95? They, as well as leaders outside the home, are more likely than average to describe themselves as entrepreneurs—a reminder to us that preparing connected Christian leaders must involve vocationally discipling young people across a range of callings, including entrepreneurship.

A second challenge is that **we lack effective pipelines, processes and models to form young leaders.** Based on U.S. data collected over three decades, we know that institutions in general and churches in particular are performing below "replacement levels" when it comes to identifying and preparing new leaders. As an example, the median age of Protestant senior pastors in the U.S. today is 54, compared to 44 in the early '90s—the whole set of church leaders is aging. Furthermore, only one in seven rates him- or herself as "excellent" when it comes to mentoring younger leaders (14%).[29] For a variety of reasons, older pastors are staying in the pulpit longer—which, of course, has some upsides (maturity being chief among them). But if we're not making room for younger leaders today, they won't be around tomorrow. And a related insight: If we're not giving young people opportunities to make us look bad (while praying they make us look good!), we're not giving them actual opportunities to lead. We're patronizing them. Far too often, this generation is more willing to be challenged than the Church is ready to challenge them.

I am so concerned about a looming shortage of Christian leaders for pastoral and other vocations that Barna is making this a major area of inquiry over the coming decade. We want to know, for the sake of the Church's future: *What environments and practices nurture potential and activate leaders?*

One of the clear imperatives of our research with Millennials and Gen Z is the need for more holistic forms of leadership development. We must invest in the connected generation, not to bring about what we think the world needs, but so they are prepared for what God is calling *them* to courageously undertake in this time of rein-vention and hope, skepticism and transparency.

Each new generation of young leaders is the new wineskin of God's purposes.

The Role Churches Play

So how are churches contributing to the development of leaders? For one thing, there are millions in the connected generation who consider themselves to be leaders in their church or faith community. It's a relatively small slice of the total population, but one in 11 says they are a leader in their

HOW CHURCHES DEVELOP LEADERS

"Which of the following, if any, have you experienced in your church, parish, or faith community?"

● All churchgoers   ◑ Leaders (outside the home)   ● Resilient disciples

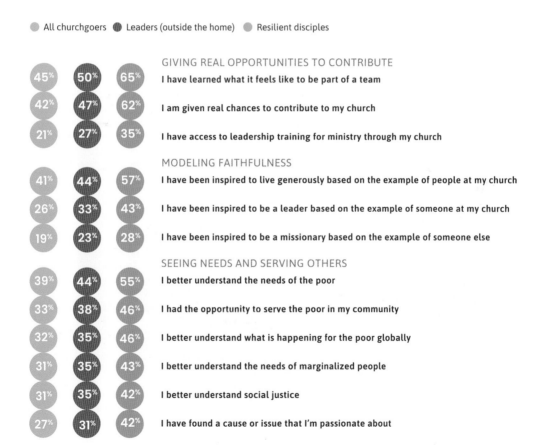

GIVING REAL OPPORTUNITIES TO CONTRIBUTE
45% 50% 65% I have learned what it feels like to be part of a team
42% 47% 62% I am given real chances to contribute to my church
21% 27% 35% I have access to leadership training for ministry through my church

MODELING FAITHFULNESS
41% 44% 57% I have been inspired to live generously based on the example of people at my church
26% 33% 43% I have been inspired to be a leader based on the example of someone at my church
19% 23% 28% I have been inspired to be a missionary based on the example of someone else

SEEING NEEDS AND SERVING OTHERS
39% 44% 55% I better understand the needs of the poor
33% 38% 46% I had the opportunity to serve the poor in my community
32% 35% 46% I better understand what is happening for the poor globally
31% 35% 43% I better understand the needs of marginalized people
31% 35% 42% I better understand social justice
27% 31% 42% I have found a cause or issue that I'm passionate about

n=4,091 adults ages 18 to 35 who identify as Christian and have attended church in the last six months, December 4, 2018–February 15, 2019.

community of faith (9%). Among resilient disciples, the ratio is two in five (39%). More young adults in majority Christian climates (13%), especially in the global South (23% Africa, 10% Latin America / South America), report serving as leaders in their church.

We asked churchgoing young adults about three different domains of leadership development: (1) opportunities to contribute, (2) models of faithfulness (how they've been inspired by their church relationships) and (3) seeing needs and serving others. The table shows a mix of positive results and room for growth. Churches are most effective at

Leaders & Connectivity

A young adult's perception of themselves as a leader outside the home is correlated with stronger connectivity than those who don't think of themselves that way. Whichever way causation runs—do leaders maintain stronger connections, or do connected people feel more confident in their leadership?—supporting the global, relational, forward-looking and outward-oriented connectivity of the connected generation will strengthen emerging leaders, as well.

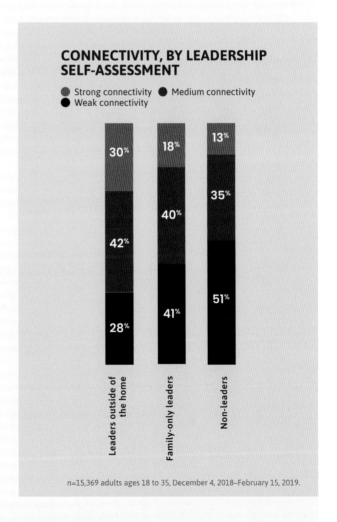

CONNECTIVITY, BY LEADERSHIP SELF-ASSESSMENT

● Strong connectivity ● Medium connectivity
● Weak connectivity

Leaders outside of the home: 30% / 42% / 28%
Family-only leaders: 18% / 40% / 41%
Non-leaders: 13% / 35% / 51%

n=15,369 adults ages 18 to 35, December 4, 2018–February 15, 2019.

giving young adults chances to "feel like part of a team," to be inspired to "live generously based on the example of others in my church" and to "better understand the needs of the poor." Those who are self-described leaders are more likely to take advantage of the opportunities offered by their church; resilient disciples are even more likely, which reflects the central role churches play in their personal development.

The connected generation is looking for the Church to provide real, tangible, meaningful opportunities for development. They want the church to be a laboratory of leadership, not just a place for spirituality. They want their faith to intersect the realities of life and, as budding Christian leaders, they want to address real life issues.

A Vision for Connected Leaders

What kind of leaders, entrepreneurs, activists and influencers are we hoping to be—and hoping young Christians will become? Here are four aspirations, whether we are part of the connected generation or simply cheering them on.[30]

We aspire to be and to form leaders who are:

Connected to God. Our identity is grounded in Jesus and we bring a God-centered presence to a self-centered age.

Connected to ourselves. We are humble, sacrificial people of peace. We reject wrong ideas about leadership and influence that say our worth is what we create and our influence equals the size of our platform. We are conscious of the relentless pull toward anxiety and freneticism and make deliberate choices to live in sync with an unruffled, unharried, Godward rhythm.

YOUNG ADULTS WANT THE CHURCH TO BE A LABORATORY OF LEADERSHIP, NOT JUST A PLACE FOR SPIRITUALITY

Connected to others. We are emotionally connected to others in our communities and in our households. We have a healthy connection to those we lead, which is neither cold and detached nor codependently enmeshed.

Connected to the world. We are informed about the major problems facing societies, personally impacted by the needs of others, and seeking opportunities to serve as agents of godly change. We are courageous and empowered to seek God-honoring solutions.

Even as the world spins toward an uncertain future, these kinds of people can make a difference—as God intends all leaders to do. ⬤

UNDERSTANDING RELUCTANT LEADERS

HOW THEY SEE THEMSELVES

Non-leaders lack confidence in themselves or their opportunities and struggle to feel support from others.

● Leaders outside the home ● Non-leaders

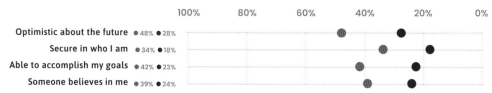

	100%	80%	60%	40%	20%	0%
Optimistic about the future ● 48% ● 28%						
Secure in who I am ● 34% ● 18%						
Able to accomplish my goals ● 42% ● 23%						
Someone believes in me ● 39% ● 24%						

HOW THEY SEE LEADERSHIP

Non-leaders appear less invested—and feel less included—in conversations about the state of leadership today.

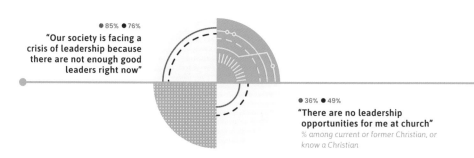

● 85% ● 76%
"Our society is facing a crisis of leadership because there are not enough good leaders right now"

● 36% ● 49%
"There are no leadership opportunities for me at church"
% among current or former Christian, or know a Christian

Issues such as gender inequality are of greater concern to this group, perhaps because non-leaders are more likely to be female (57%, compared to 43% of leaders outside the home).

WHAT DO YOU THINK ARE THE BIGGEST CHALLENGES TO LEADERSHIP TODAY?

○ Leaders outside the home ○ Non-leaders

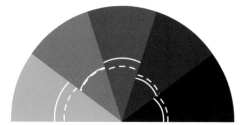

○ 55% ○ 44% ● **Everyone is too busy and distracted**

○ 42% ○ 41% ● **Society is becoming so fragmented into different groups that it is hard to lead**

○ 47% ○ 38% ● **Everyone has to compete now in a global marketplace**

○ 31% ○ 35% ● **Racial inequality**

○ 29% ○ 34% ● **Gender inequality**

The viewpoints of 18–35-year-olds who don't (yet) consider themselves to be leaders reveal room for growth and opportunities to champion the potential of the connected generation.

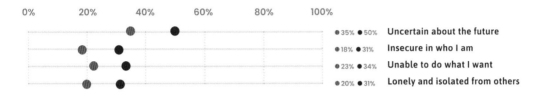

● 35% ● 50%	**Uncertain about the future**
● 18% ● 31%	**Insecure in who I am**
● 23% ● 34%	**Unable to do what I want**
● 20% ● 31%	**Lonely and isolated from others**

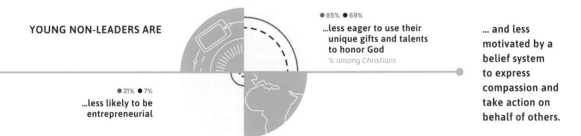

YOUNG NON-LEADERS ARE

● 85% ● 69%
...less eager to use their unique gifts and talents to honor God
% among Christians

... and less motivated by a belief system to express compassion and take action on behalf of others.

● 21% ● 7%
...less likely to be entrepreneurial

"BECAUSE OF MY BELIEFS, IT'S IMPORTANT THAT I ..."

○ 56% ◔ 42% ●	**Am concerned about the welfare of others**
○ 58% ◔ 37% ●	**Give of my time to help others in need**
○ 54% ◔ 36% ●	**Stand up against injustices against individuals or groups**
○ 53% ◔ 33% ●	**Stand up against corruption**
○ 49% ◔ 30% ●	**Give of my own resources to help others in need**

n=12,478 adults ages 18 to 35 who identify either as leaders outside the home or as non-leaders, December 4, 2018–February 15, 2019.

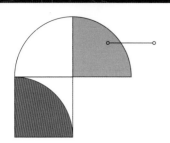

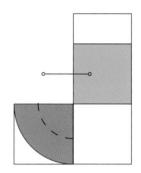

Connect the Dots:
Potential for Impact

REFLECTIONS AND NEXT STEPS
INSPIRED BY THE RESEARCH

See the whole.

- Four out of five practicing Christians say they want to honor God in the work they do, but very few are involved in their church specifically for career development. Vocational discipleship is a massive need for young adults and an enormous opportunity for churches to make resilient disciples.
- The connected generation has global concerns—corruption, climate change, extreme poverty—and eight in 10 agree there is a lack of effective leadership. Many want to be part of solutions but aren't sure how.
- There is a strong entrepreneurial streak in the next generation that should inspire older leaders to invest not only capital but also time, attention, prayer and emotional resources.

Take time to pray.

- For this generation to answer God's call to honor him in all they do; for God to call and equip young leaders to meet the world's toughest challenges.
- For healing of rifts between generations: revealing to older believers how God is working among young disciples in your community and showing young believers how to trust the help and influence of older mentors.
- For your community to prepare and launch young leaders in every sphere of life, but especially in the Church; for you to make time to know, equip and activate tomorrow's leaders.

Create what's next.

- *Listen.* Young adults may still be developing a vocabulary of leadership and are learning to articulate their priorities and perspectives. A receptive audience might contribute to clarity. If you're in this generation, articulate what you think is important. If you're working with this generation, be open to their influence.
- *Think.* What is your theology of work and vocation? How can you and your community vocationally disciple the connected generation?
- *Act.* Begin mentoring and investing in the next generation. Leaders raise up leaders.

Conclusion

In more ways than one, these pages represent a multi-cultural, multi-generational, international effort, on behalf of the teams at Barna and World Vision as well as a network of experts, reviewers and contributors. In addition to the 15,000+ respondents from 25 countries who participated in our study, people from around the globe have come together to support and inform this work and ask big questions of a generation who are full of questions themselves. It's been a thrill and a challenge to not only mine the data from such a vast study but also to turn it into something helpful and maybe even hopeful for the Church.

Ultimately, looking back on many years of related research, this study has confirmed several aspects of our paradoxical profile of Millennials and now Gen Z—connected but alone, ambitious but anxious, open-minded but skeptical. At the same time, it's significantly nuanced our understanding of how these young adults see themselves, engage with spirituality and perceive the world at this present moment. At

a high level, the story is this: There are significant hurdles to the stability, well-being and beliefs of today's teens, twentysomethings and thirtysomethings. Thirty-eight percent of respondents are categorized by Barna as having weak connectivity and struggle to find their place, their people or their purpose. But where connectivity is strong, something has *clicked*. Faith thrives. Community is present. Vocation, calling and potential are nurtured. Justice and corruption are confronted. These are links to note and learn from, whatever your proximity to this age range, wherever you live.

Even if this report leaves you with an enhanced general image of 18–35-year-olds—where they are now and where they are headed—we also recognize that your own age, spiritual heritage, national climate or cultural identity are just beyond the frame, inevitably filtering the way you view the findings. No single resource could speak to all backgrounds and considerations in full, though we hope that as you digest the data, read the Q&As and even follow prompts from the Connect the Dots pages, you might be able to distill the research for your day-to-day reality. Further, as there is still much more to learn about these young adults, specifically at a country-specific level, we encourage you to stay in touch at **theconnectedgeneration.com**, where we will continue to roll out findings and other resources, analysis, interviews and research-backed recommendations from *The Connected Generation* study.

Our vision is that this research will help you as you help an influential generation address (not just quiet) doubts and anxieties and become resilient, courageous contributors to neighborhoods, nonprofits, workplaces, churches, even nations. Join us in continuing to listen to, pray for and equip teens and young adults in your sphere.

Faith *for the* Future

What We Are Learning About Resilient Discipleship from the Connected Generation

Watch the webcast and extended interviews with contributors at **TheConnectedGeneration.com**.

The Connected Generation project launched with the Faith for the Future webcast, a live, free event where leaders from Barna and World Vision revealed the main findings—some sobering, some hopeful—uncovered by this global study. The team was joined by panels of experts and ministers, as well as viewers from 88 countries and six continents, to help answer: **How do we turn this research into action?**

"The baton of faith is in our hands. We get to carry this baton to the next generation. But there's always an exchange zone."
Christine Caine

"I cannot set others up for success if I have a filtered life. The best way I can set others up for success is to be honest about my failures."
Brianna Parker

"There is a resistance toward anyone with all the answers. I think evangelism looks like listening, invitation, hospitality, gathering around the table."
Jason Ballard

"What would it look like to leverage a platform for the sake of the kingdom? Having social media followers is great, but where are we leading people?"
Sam Collier

"I don't think this generation's desire to contribute is superficial. It's to see the real-world experiences— the injustices, the suffering, the anxiety—addressed within the context of where we work and worship."
Amanda Bowman

"For the younger generation, discipleship is about finding those people who really walk with the Lord and sticking with them and being resilient, even when your own feelings and opinions are completely different."
Francis Chan

"We don't have an understanding about what it means to go deep and what it means to have a theology of the marathon."
Eugene Cho

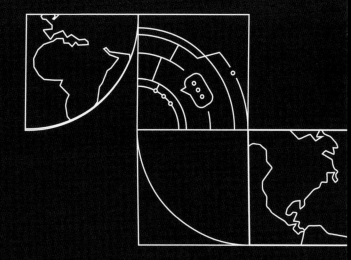

COUNTRY PROFILES

Key measures of faith and connectivity
among 18–35-year-olds in 25 countries

Refer to the glossary of key terms on page 12 for all definitions.

OVERALL FAITH PROFILE:

AUSTRALIA

RELIGIOUS CLIMATE: SECULAR

CONNECTIVITY (OVERALL)

STRONG · **20%** · MEDIUM · **39%** · WEAK · **40%**

WARMTH TOWARD RELIGION

"Religion is good for people" — "Religion is harmful to people"

| 20% | 25% | 25% | 18% | 12% |

"Religion is important to society" — "Religion is a detriment to society"

| 18% | 21% | 28% | 21% | 11% |

Globally Connected

60% "I feel connected to people around the world"

80% "Events around the world matter to me"

Relationally Connected

33% "I often feel deeply cared for by those around me"

30% "I often feel like someone believes in me"

RELATIONSHIP TO RELIGION

"The Church is good for people" — "The Church is harmful to people"

| 18% | 26% | 29% | 15% | 12% |

"The Church is important to society" — "The Church is a detriment to society"

| 16% | 24% | 29% | 17% | 13% |

Attendance of Religious Respondents

21% Weekly

17% At least once a month, but not weekly

37% Infrequently, but occasionally

24% Never

Do you feel like the Christian Church is making a difference on issues such as poverty and justice?

12% Definitely

40% Probably

32% Probably not

16% Definitely not

"My religious faith is very important in my life today"

47%

"Because of my beliefs, it is important that I

52% ... am concerned about the welfare of others"

48% ... give of my time to help others in need"

46% ... stand up against injustices against individuals or groups"

OVERALL FAITH PROFILE:

AUSTRIA

RELIGIOUS CLIMATE: SECULAR

CONNECTIVITY (OVERALL)

STRONG **21%** MEDIUM **40%** WEAK **38%**

WARMTH TOWARD RELIGION

"Religion is good for people"   "Religion is harmful to people"

| 19% | 31% | 26% | 16% | 9% |

"Religion is important to society"   "Religion is a detriment to society"

| 14% | 28% | 28% | 21% | 9% |

Globally Connected

45% "I feel connected to people around the world"

63% "Events around the world matter to me"

Relationally Connected

51% "I often feel deeply cared for by those around me"

32% "I often feel like someone believes in me"

RELATIONSHIP TO RELIGION

"The Church is good for people"   "The Church is harmful to people"

| 14% | 29% | 34% | 14% | 10% |

"The Church is important to society"   "The Church is a detriment to society"

| 13% | 25% | 35% | 17% | 10% |

Attendance of Religious Respondents

9% Weekly

11% At least once a month, but not weekly

56% Infrequently, but occasionally

24% Never

Do you feel like the Christian Church is making a difference on issues such as poverty and justice?

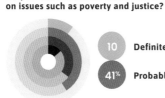

10 Definitely

41% Probably

35% Probably not

14% Definitely not

"My religious faith is very important in my life today"

34%

"Because of my beliefs, it is important that I

38% ... am concerned about the welfare of others"

36% ... stand up against injustices against individuals or groups"

24% ... give of my time to help others in"

OVERALL FAITH PROFILE:

BRAZIL

RELIGIOUS CLIMATE: CHRISTIAN

CONNECTIVITY (OVERALL)

STRONG **26**% → MEDIUM **41**% WEAK **33**%

WARMTH TOWARD RELIGION

"Religion is good for people" — **"Religion is harmful to people"**

50%	26%	11%	8%	6%

"Religion is important to society" — **"Religion is a detriment to society"**

47%	28%	11%	8%	7%

RELATIONSHIP TO RELIGION

"The Church is good for people" — **"The Church is harmful to people"**

49%	28%	11%	7%	5%

"The Church is important to society" — **"The Church is a detriment to society"**

47%	27%	12%	8%	6%

Globally Connected

64% "I feel connected to people around the world"

71% "Events around the world matter to me"

Relationally Connected

26% "I often feel deeply cared for by those around me"

32% "I often feel like someone believes in me"

Attendance of Religious Respondents

41% Weekly

23% At least once a month, but not weekly

23% Infrequently, but occasionally

13% Never

Do you feel like the Christian Church is making a difference on issues such as poverty and justice?

23% Definitely
47% Probably
21% Probably not
8% Definitely not

"My religious faith is very important in my life today"

83%

"Because of my beliefs, it is important that I

68% ... am concerned about the welfare of others"

58% ... give of my time to help others in need"

56% ... stand up against corruption"

OVERALL FAITH PROFILE:

CANADA

RELIGIOUS CLIMATE: SECULAR

CONNECTIVITY (OVERALL)

STRONG **25%** — MEDIUM **37%** — WEAK **39%**

WARMTH TOWARD RELIGION

"Religion is good for people" — "Religion is harmful to people"

| 24% | 29% | 24% | 14% | 9% |

"Religion is important to society" — "Religion is a detriment to society"

| 19% | 26% | 27% | 16% | 11% |

Globally Connected

56% "I feel connected to people around the world"

80% "Events around the world matter to me"

Relationally Connected

35% "I often feel deeply cared for by those around me"

31% "I often feel like someone believes in me"

RELATIONSHIP TO RELIGION

"The Church is good for people" — "The Church is harmful to people"

| 23% | 26% | 28% | 13% | 10% |

"The Church is important to society" — "The Church is a detriment to society"

| 21% | 24% | 29% | 15% | 11% |

Attendance of Religious Respondents

22% Weekly

16% At least once a month, but not weekly

37% Infrequently, but occasionally

25% Never

Do you feel like the Christian Church is making a difference on issues such as poverty and justice?

 14% Definitely

42% Probably

31% Probably not

14% Definitely not

"My religious faith is very important in my life today"

50%

"Because of my beliefs, it is important that I

51% ... am concerned about the welfare of others"

49% ... give of my time to help others in need"

44% ... stand up against injustices against individuals or groups"

OVERALL FAITH PROFILE:
CHILE

RELIGIOUS CLIMATE: CHRISTIAN

CONNECTIVITY (OVERALL)

STRONG **37%** MEDIUM **43%** WEAK **20%**

WARMTH TOWARD RELIGION

"Religion is good for people" — "Religion is harmful to people"

| 24% | 30% | 18% | 18% | 10% |

"Religion is important to society" — "Religion is a detriment to society"

| 23% | 26% | 15% | 23% | 12% |

Globally Connected

73% "I feel connected to people around the world"

91% "Events around the world matter to me"

Relationally Connected

30% "I often feel deeply cared for by those around me"

46% "I often feel like someone believes in me"

RELATIONSHIP TO RELIGION

"The Church is good for people" — "The Church is harmful to people"

| 23% | 23% | 23% | 18% | 12% |

"The Church is important to society" — "The Church is a detriment to society"

| 20% | 27% | 19% | 20% | 14% |

Attendance of Religious Respondents

18% Weekly

22% At least once a month, but not weekly

30% Infrequently, but occasionally

30% Never

Do you feel like the Christian Church is making a difference on issues such as poverty and justice?

11% Definitely

27% Probably

31% Probably not

30% Definitely not

"My religious faith is very important in my life today"

60%

"Because of my beliefs, it is important that I

59% ... am concerned about the welfare of others"

46% ... stand up against injustices against individuals or groups"

43% ... stand up against corruption"

OVERALL FAITH PROFILE:

COLOMBIA

RELIGIOUS CLIMATE: CHRISTIAN

CONNECTIVITY (OVERALL)

STRONG **37%** → MEDIUM **39%** WEAK **24%**

WARMTH TOWARD RELIGION

"Religion is good for people" — "Religion is harmful to people"

34%	28%	15%	13%	11%

"Religion is important to society" — "Religion is a detriment to society"

30%	28%	17%	15%	10%

Globally Connected

66% "I feel connected to people around the world"

84% "Events around the world matter to me"

Relationally Connected

30% "I often feel deeply cared for by those around me"

39% "I often feel like someone believes in me"

RELATIONSHIP TO RELIGION

"The Church is good for people" — "The Church is harmful to people"

33%	28%	18%	14%	7%

"The Church is important to society" — "The Church is a detriment to society"

33%	30%	15%	14%	8%

Attendance of Religious Respondents

32% Weekly

32% At least once a month, but not weekly

27% Infrequently, but occasionally

9% Never

Do you feel like the Christian Church is making a difference on issues such as poverty and justice?

17% Definitely

40% Probably

26% Probably not

17% Definitely not

"My religious faith is very important in my life today"

75%

"Because of my beliefs, it is important that I

62% ... am concerned about the welfare of others"

50% ... give of my time to help others in need"

43% ... stand up against corruption"

OVERALL FAITH PROFILE:
GERMANY

RELIGIOUS CLIMATE:
SECULAR

CONNECTIVITY (OVERALL)

STRONG **18**% — MEDIUM **38**% — WEAK **44**%

WARMTH TOWARD RELIGION

"Religion is good
for people"   "Religion is harmful
                                                to people"

| 11% | 30% | 27% | 19% | 12% |

"Religion is important
to society"   "Religion is a
                                               detriment to society"

| 11% | 27% | 27% | 21% | 15% |

Globally Connected

48% "I feel connected to people around the world"

63% "Events around the world matter to me"

Relationally Connected

43% "I often feel deeply cared for by those around me"

29% "I often feel like someone believes in me"

RELATIONSHIP TO RELIGION

"The Church is
good for people"   "The Church is
                                               harmful to people"

| 12% | 32% | 28% | 16% | 12% |

"The Church is
important to society"   "The Church is a
                                               detriment to society"

| 11% | 29% | 29% | 19% | 13% |

Attendance of Religious Respondents

7% Weekly

18% At least once a month, but not weekly

49% Infrequently, but occasionally

27% Never

Do you feel like the Christian Church is making a difference on issues such as poverty and justice?

11% Definitely

42% Probably

35% Probably not

12% Definitely not

"My religious faith
is very important
in my life today"

32%

"Because of my beliefs, it is important that I

39% ... stand up against injustices against individuals or groups"

36% ... am concerned about the welfare of others"

24% ... give of my time to help others in need"

OVERALL FAITH PROFILE:
GHANA

RELIGIOUS CLIMATE: CHRISTIAN

CONNECTIVITY (OVERALL)

STRONG **30%** MEDIUM **39%** WEAK **31%**

WARMTH TOWARD RELIGION

"Religion is good for people" | "Religion is harmful to people"

70% 11% 11% 4% 5%

"Religion is important to society" | "Religion is a detriment to society"

67% 10% 12% 5% 5%

Globally Connected

67% "I feel connected to people around the world"

89% "Events around the world matter to me"

Relationally Connected

30% "I often feel deeply cared for by those around me"

36% "I often feel like someone believes in me"

RELATIONSHIP TO RELIGION

"The Church is good for people" | "The Church is harmful to people"

72% 12% 11% 2% 3%

"The Church is important to society" | "The Church is a detriment to society"

69% 14% 11% 1% 4%

Attendance of Religious Respondents

71% Weekly

16% At least once a month, but not weekly

10% Infrequently, but occasionally

4% Never

Do you feel like the Christian Church is making a difference on issues such as poverty and justice?

29% Definitely
41% Probably
20% Probably not
10% Definitely not

"My religious faith is very important in my life today"

94%

"Because of my beliefs, it is important that I

77% ... stand up against corruption"

76% ... give of my time to help others in need"

72% ... am concerned about the welfare of others"

OVERALL FAITH PROFILE:

INDIA

RELIGIOUS CLIMATE: MULTI-FAITH

CONNECTIVITY (OVERALL)

STRONG **21%** — MEDIUM **46%** — WEAK **33%**

WARMTH TOWARD RELIGION

"Religion is good for people" | "Religion is harmful to people"

| 29% | 19% | 29% | 12% | 11% |

"Religion is important to society" | "Religion is a detriment to society"

| 24% | 21% | 30% | 14% | 11% |

Globally Connected

76% "I feel connected to people around the world"

82% "Events around the world matter to me"

Relationally Connected

31% "I often feel deeply cared for by those around me"

33% "I often feel like someone believes in me"

RELATIONSHIP TO RELIGION

"The Church is good for people" | "The Church is harmful to people"

| 35% | 24% | 27% | 7% | 6% |

"The Church is important to society" | "The Church is a detriment to society"

| 23% | 27% | 34% | 10% | 6% |

Attendance of Religious Respondents

24% Weekly

36% At least once a month, but not weekly

32% Infrequently, but occasionally

8% Never

Do you feel like the Christian Church is making a difference on issues such as poverty and justice?

18% Definitely
46% Probably
25% Probably not
10% Definitely not

"My religious faith is very important in my life today"

84%

"Because of my beliefs, it is important that I

57% ... give of my time to help others in need."

57% ... stand up against corruption"

46% ... stand up against injustices against individuals or groups"

OVERALL FAITH PROFILE:
INDONESIA

RELIGIOUS CLIMATE: MULTI-FAITH

CONNECTIVITY (OVERALL)

STRONG **22%** → MEDIUM **40%** ← WEAK **38%**

WARMTH TOWARD RELIGION

"Religion is good for people" / "Religion is harmful to people"

| 68% | 10% | 10% | 2% | 10% |

"Religion is important to society" / "Religion is a detriment to society"

| 65% | 13% | 9% | 3% | 11% |

Globally Connected

61% "I feel connected to people around the world"

76% "Events around the world matter to me"

Relationally Connected

38% "I often feel deeply cared for by those around me"

21% "I often feel like someone believes in me"

RELATIONSHIP TO RELIGION

"The Church is good for people" / "The Church is harmful to people"

| 28% | 21% | 34% | 8% | 8% |

"The Church is important to society" / "The Church is a detriment to society"

| 26% | 22% | 36% | 8% | 8% |

Attendance of Religious Respondents

57% Weekly

23% At least once a month, but not weekly

14% Infrequently, but occasionally

6% Never

Do you feel like the Christian Church is making a difference on issues such as poverty and justice?

9% Definitely
46% Probably
28% Probably not
17% Definitely not

"My religious faith is very important in my life today"

97%

"Because of my beliefs, it is important that I

71% ... give of my time to help others in need"

60% ... give of my own resources to help others in need"

55% ... am concerned about the welfare of others"

OVERALL FAITH PROFILE:
KENYA

RELIGIOUS CLIMATE: CHRISTIAN

CONNECTIVITY (OVERALL)

STRONG **36%**   MEDIUM **40%**   WEAK **24%**

WARMTH TOWARD RELIGION

"Religion is good for people"   "Religion is harmful to people"

| 76% | 14% | 7% | 2% | 2% |

"Religion is important to society"   "Religion is a detriment to society"

| 73% | 15% | 6% | 2% | 4% |

Globally Connected

70% "I feel connected to people around the world"

88% "Events around the world matter to me"

Relationally Connected

34% "I often feel deeply cared for by those around me"

41% "I often feel like someone believes in me"

RELATIONSHIP TO RELIGION

"The Church is good for people"   "The Church is harmful to people"

| 77% | 12% | 7% | 1% | 3% |

"The Church is important to society"   "The Church is a detriment to society"

| 77% | 15% | 4% | 1% | 3% |

Attendance of Religious Respondents

62% Weekly

24% At least once a month, but not weekly

12% Infrequently, but occasionally

2% Never

Do you feel like the Christian Church is making a difference on issues such as poverty and justice?

35% Definitely   **9%** Probably not

47% Probably   **8%** Definitely not

"My religious faith is very important in my life today"

96%

"Because of my beliefs, it is important that I

79% ... stand up against corruption"

75% ... give of my time to help others in need"

75% ... stand up against injustices against individuals or groups"

OVERALL FAITH PROFILE:

MALAYSIA

RELIGIOUS CLIMATE: MULTI-FAITH

CONNECTIVITY (OVERALL)

STRONG **15%** — MEDIUM **40%** — WEAK **46%**

WARMTH TOWARD RELIGION

"Religion is good for people" — "Religion is harmful to people"

| 63% | 15% | 13% | 4% | 5% |

"Religion is important to society" — "Religion is a detriment to society"

| 59% | 19% | 13% | 6% | 4% |

Globally Connected

60% "I feel connected to people around the world"

68% "Events around the world matter to me"

Relationally Connected

26% "I often feel deeply cared for by those around me"

30% "I often feel like someone believes in me"

RELATIONSHIP TO RELIGION

"The Church is good for people" — "The Church is harmful to people"

| 27% | 23% | 31% | 10% | 10% |

"The Church is important to society" — "The Church is a detriment to society"

| 23% | 21% | 34% | 10% | 12% |

Attendance of Religious Respondents

28% Weekly
27% At least once a month, but not weekly
38% Infrequently, but occasionally
7% Never

Do you feel like the Christian Church is making a difference on issues such as poverty and justice?

9% Definitely
56% Probably
23% Probably not
12% Definitely not

"My religious faith is very important in my life today"

94%

"Because of my beliefs, it is important that I

63% ... give of my time to help others in need"
52% ... stand up against corruption"
49% ... give of my resources to help others in need"

OVERALL FAITH PROFILE:
MEXICO

RELIGIOUS CLIMATE: CHRISTIAN

CONNECTIVITY (OVERALL)

STRONG **28%** — MEDIUM **46%** — WEAK **26%**

WARMTH TOWARD RELIGION

"Religion is good for people" | "Religion is harmful to people"

| 31% | 30% | 21% | 10% | 8% |

"Religion is important to society" | "Religion is a detriment to society"

| 27% | 31% | 22% | 13% | 7% |

Globally Connected

65% "I feel connected to people around the world"

92% "Events around the world matter to me"

Relationally Connected

22% "I often feel deeply cared for by those around me"

36% "I often feel like someone believes in me"

RELATIONSHIP TO RELIGION

"The Church is good for people" | "The Church is harmful to people"

| 29% | 31% | 23% | 10% | 8% |

"The Church is important to society" | "The Church is a detriment to society"

| 27% | 28% | 26% | 11% | 9% |

Attendance of Religious Respondents

24% Weekly

30% At least once a month, but not weekly

36% Infrequently, but occasionally

10% Never

Do you feel like the Christian Church is making a difference on issues such as poverty and justice?

19% Definitely
37% Probably
26% Probably not
18% Definitely not

"My religious faith is very important in my life today"

76%

"Because of my beliefs, it is important that I

52% ... am concerned about the welfare of others"

40% ... give of my time to help others in need"

37% ... stand up against corruption"

OVERALL FAITH PROFILE:

NEW ZEALAND

RELIGIOUS CLIMATE: SECULAR

CONNECTIVITY (OVERALL)

STRONG **22%** MEDIUM **35%** WEAK **43%**

WARMTH TOWARD RELIGION

"Religion is good for people" — "Religion is harmful to people"

| 16% | 27% | 29% | 17% | 10% |

"Religion is important to society" — "Religion is a detriment to society"

| 16% | 25% | 31% | 18% | 12% |

Globally Connected

51% "I feel connected to people around the world"

74% "Events around the world matter to me"

Relationally Connected

33% "I often feel deeply cared for by those around me"

30% "I often feel like someone believes in me"

RELATIONSHIP TO RELIGION

"The Church is good for people" — "The Church is harmful to people"

| 18% | 28% | 32% | 12% | 10% |

"The Church is important to society" — "The Church is a detriment to society"

| 17% | 23% | 34% | 17% | 10% |

Attendance of Religious Respondents

29% Weekly

19% At least once a month, but not weekly

27% Infrequently, but occasionally

26% Never

Do you feel like the Christian Church is making a difference on issues such as poverty and justice?

10% Definitely
42% Probably
33% Probably not
16% Definitely not

"My religious faith is very important in my life today"

45%

"Because of my beliefs, it is important that I

48% ... give of my time to help others in need"

45% ... am concerned about the welfare of others"

44% ... stand up against injustices against individuals or groups"

44% ... stand up against corruption"

OVERALL FAITH PROFILE:

NIGERIA

RELIGIOUS CLIMATE: CHRISTIAN

CONNECTIVITY (OVERALL)

STRONG — **32%** — MEDIUM — **42%** — WEAK — **25%**

WARMTH TOWARD RELIGION

"Religion is good for people" → "Religion is harmful to people"

| 67% | 13% | 9% | 4% | 7% |

"Religion is important to society" → "Religion is a detriment to society"

| 65% | 11% | 10% | 5% | 8% |

Globally Connected

69% "I feel connected to people around the world"

88% "Events around the world matter to me"

Relationally Connected

35% "I often feel deeply cared for by those around me"

41% "I often feel like someone believes in me"

RELATIONSHIP TO RELIGION

"The Church is good for people" → "The Church is harmful to people"

| 67% | 13% | 11% | 3% | 5% |

"The Church is important to society" → "The Church is a detriment to society"

| 65% | 13% | 12% | 4% | 6% |

Attendance of Religious Respondents

74% Weekly

14% At least once a month, but not weekly

10% Infrequently, but occasionally

3% Never

Do you feel like the Christian Church is making a difference on issues such as poverty and justice?

35% Definitely

40% Probably

16% Probably not

9% Definitely not

"My religious faith is very important in my life today"

93%

"Because of my beliefs, it is important that I ...

73% ... give of my time to help others in need"

72% ... stand up against corruption"

71% ... am concerned about the welfare of others"

OVERALL FAITH PROFILE:

PHILIPPINES

RELIGIOUS CLIMATE: CHRISTIAN

CONNECTIVITY (OVERALL)

STRONG — **29%** — MEDIUM — **48%** — WEAK — **24%**

WARMTH TOWARD RELIGION

"Religion is good for people" / "Religion is harmful to people"

| 39% | 22% | 26% | 5% | 9% |

"Religion is important to society" / "Religion is a detriment to society"

| 40% | 21% | 22% | 8% | 9% |

Globally Connected

68% "I feel connected to people around the world"

86% "Events around the world matter to me"

Relationally Connected

33% "I often feel deeply cared for by those around me"

40% "I often feel like someone believes in me"

RELATIONSHIP TO RELIGION

"The Church is good for people" / "The Church is harmful to people"

| 42% | 21% | 24% | 7% | 6% |

"The Church is important to society" / "The Church is a detriment to society"

| 41% | 21% | 23% | 7% | 8% |

Attendance of Religious Respondents

43% Weekly

29% At least once a month, but not weekly

23% Infrequently, but occasionally

6% Never

Do you feel like the Christian Church is making a difference on issues such as poverty and justice?

27% Definitely
53% Probably
14% Probably not
6% Definitely not

"My religious faith is very important in my life today"

89%

"Because of my beliefs, it is important that I

64% ... give of my time to help others in need"

48% ... am concerned about the welfare of others"

46% ... stand up against injustices against individuals or groups"

ACTIVATING

OVERALL FAITH PROFILE:

ROMANIA

RELIGIOUS CLIMATE: CHRISTIAN

CONNECTIVITY (OVERALL)

STRONG — 19% — MEDIUM — 47% — WEAK — 34%

WARMTH TOWARD RELIGION

"Religion is good for people" / "Religion is harmful to people"

| 45% | 26% | 16% | 9% | 4% |

"Religion is important to society" / "Religion is a detriment to society"

| 43% | 29% | 11% | 11% | 6% |

Globally Connected

55% "I feel connected to people around the world"

72% "Events around the world matter to me"

Relationally Connected

21% "I often feel deeply cared for by those around me"

36 "I often feel like someone believes in me"

RELATIONSHIP TO RELIGION

"The Church is good for people" / "The Church is harmful to people"

| 41% | 28% | 16% | 11% | 4% |

"The Church is important to society" / "The Church is a detriment to society"

| 39% | 31% | 15% | 10% | 6% |

Attendance of Religious Respondents

13% Weekly

21% At least once a month, but not weekly

55% Infrequently, but occasionally

11% Never

Do you feel like the Christian Church is making a difference on issues such as poverty and justice?

22% Definitely

37% Probably

23% Probably not

18% Definitely not

"My religious faith is very important in my life today"

71%

"Because of my beliefs, it is important that I

68% ... stand up against corruption"

46% ... stand up against injustices against individuals or groups"

45% ... give of my time to help others in need"

OVERALL FAITH PROFILE:
SINGAPORE

RELIGIOUS CLIMATE: MULTI-FAITH

CONNECTIVITY (OVERALL)

STRONG **15%** MEDIUM **38%** WEAK **46%**

WARMTH TOWARD RELIGION

"Religion is good for people" .... **"Religion is harmful to people"**

| 36% | 26% | 25% | 7% | 6% |

"Religion is important to society" .... **"Religion is a detriment to society"**

| 27% | 24% | 35% | 7% | 6% |

Globally Connected

58% "I feel connected to people around the world"

71% "Events around the world matter to me"

Relationally Connected

26% "I often feel deeply cared for by those around me"

27% "I often feel like someone believes in me"

RELATIONSHIP TO RELIGION

"The Church is good for people" .... **"The Church is harmful to people"**

| 23% | 23% | 40% | 6% | 8% |

"The Church is important to society" .... **"The Church is a detriment to society"**

| 21% | 20% | 44% | 9% | 7% |

Attendance of Religious Respondents

25% Weekly

18% At least once a month, but not weekly

43% Infrequently, but occasionally

13% Never

Do you feel like the Christian Church is making a difference on issues such as poverty and justice?

11% Definitely
50% Probably
28% Probably not
11% Definitely not

"My religious faith is very important in my life today"

66%

"Because of my beliefs, it is important that I

53% ... give of my time to help others in need"

52% ... give of my own resources to help others in need"

45% ... am concerned about the welfare of others"

OVERALL FAITH PROFILE:
SOUTH AFRICA

RELIGIOUS CLIMATE: CHRISTIAN

CONNECTIVITY (OVERALL)

STRONG   **29%**   MEDIUM   **41%**   WEAK   **31%**

WARMTH TOWARD RELIGION

"Religion is good for people"   "Religion is harmful to people"

| 48% | 23% | 12% | 8% | 9% |

"Religion is important to society"   "Religion is a detriment to society"

| 46% | 24% | 15% | 8% | 7% |

Globally Connected

60% "I feel connected to people around the world"

81% "Events around the world matter to me"

Relationally Connected

36% "I often feel deeply cared for by those around me"

42% "I often feel like someone believes in me"

RELATIONSHIP TO RELIGION

"The Church is good for people"   "The Church is harmful to people"

| 50% | 23% | 13% | 7% | 7% |

"The Church is important to society"   "The Church is a detriment to society"

| 47% | 24% | 15% | 8% | 7% |

Attendance of Religious Respondents

38% Weekly

26% At least once a month, but not weekly

22% Infrequently, but occasionally

13% Never

Do you feel like the Christian Church is making a difference on issues such as poverty and justice?

24% Definitely   **21%** Probably not

42% Probably   **12%** Definitely not

"My religious faith is very important in my life today"

81%

"Because of my beliefs, it is important that I

71% ... give of my time to help others in need"

63% ... give of my own resources to help others in need"

61% ... stand up against corruption"

OVERALL FAITH PROFILE:
SOUTH KOREA

RELIGIOUS CLIMATE: CHRISTIAN

CONNECTIVITY (OVERALL)

STRONG **12%** — MEDIUM **28%** — WEAK **60%**

WARMTH TOWARD RELIGION

"Religion is good for people" / "Religion is harmful to people"

| 16% | 26% | 38% | 14% | 5% |

"Religion is important to society" / "Religion is a detriment to society"

| 15% | 17% | 45% | 17% | 6% |

Globally Connected

29% "I feel connected to people around the world"

41% "Events around the world matter to me"

Relationally Connected

31% "I often feel deeply cared for by those around me"

39% "I often feel like someone believes in me"

RELATIONSHIP TO RELIGION

"The Church is good for people" / "The Church is harmful to people"

| 14% | 18% | 45% | 12% | 11% |

"The Church is important to society" / "The Church is a detriment to society"

| 12% | 16% | 40% | 20% | 12% |

Attendance of Religious Respondents

35% Weekly

16% At least once a month, but not weekly

18% Infrequently, but occasionally

31% Never

Do you feel like the Christian Church is making a difference on issues such as poverty and justice?

0% Definitely
1% Probably
1% Probably not
97% Definitely not

"My religious faith is very important in my life today"

26%

"Because of my beliefs, it is important that I

28% ... stand up against injustices against individuals or groups"

22% ... give of my time to help others in need"

22% ... give of my resources to help others in need"

OVERALL FAITH PROFILE:
SPAIN

RELIGIOUS CLIMATE: SECULAR

CONNECTIVITY (OVERALL)

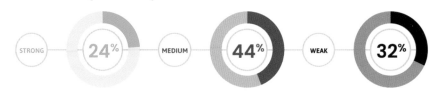

STRONG — **24**% — MEDIUM — **44**% — WEAK — **32**%

WARMTH TOWARD RELIGION

"Religion is good for people" — "Religion is harmful to people"

| 18% | 28% | 23% | 16% | 15% |

"Religion is important to society" — "Religion is a detriment to society"

| 15% | 26% | 24% | 20% | 14% |

Globally Connected

70% — "I feel connected to people around the world"

84% — "Events around the world matter to me"

Relationally Connected

26% — "I often feel deeply cared for by those around me"

28% — "I often feel like someone believes in me"

RELATIONSHIP TO RELIGION

"The Church is good for people" — "The Church is harmful to people"

| 16% | 26% | 26% | 18% | 14% |

"The Church is important to society" — "The Church is a detriment to society"

| 14% | 25% | 24% | 21% | 17% |

Attendance of Religious Respondents

12% — Weekly

20% — At least once a month, but not weekly

42% — Infrequently, but occasionally

26% — Never

Do you feel like the Christian Church is making a difference on issues such as poverty and justice?

13% Definitely

37% Probably

25% Probably not

25% Definitely not

"My religious faith is very important in my life today"

46%

"Because of my beliefs, it is important that I

55% ... am concerned about the welfare of others"

37% ... stand up against injustices against individuals or groups"

33% ... give of my time to help others in need"

OVERALL FAITH PROFILE:

SWITZERLAND

RELIGIOUS CLIMATE: SECULAR

CONNECTIVITY (OVERALL)

STRONG — **22%** — MEDIUM — **38%** — WEAK — **40%**

WARMTH TOWARD RELIGION

"Religion is good for people" .... **"Religion is harmful to people"**

| 14% | 25% | 25% | 21% | 16% |

"Religion is important to society" .... **"Religion is a detriment to society"**

| 11% | 21% | 26% | 26% | 16% |

Globally Connected

53% "I feel connected to people around the world"

64% "Events around the world matter to me"

Relationally Connected

39% "I often feel deeply cared for by those around me"

35% "I often feel like someone believes in me"

RELATIONSHIP TO RELIGION

"The Church is good for people" .... **"The Church is harmful to people"**

| 14% | 26% | 29% | 17% | 14% |

"The Church is important to society" .... **"The Church is a detriment to society"**

| 11% | 24% | 30% | 21% | 15% |

Attendance of Religious Respondents

7% Weekly

16% At least once a month, but not weekly

49% Infrequently, but occasionally

29% Never

Do you feel like the Christian Church is making a difference on issues such as poverty and justice?

11% Definitely

40% Probably

34% Probably not

16% Definitely not

"My religious faith is very important in my life today"

33%

"Because of my beliefs, it is important that I

39% ... stand up against injustices against individuals or groups"

33% ... am concerned about the welfare of others"

26% ... stand up against corruption"

OVERALL FAITH PROFILE:

TAIWAN

RELIGIOUS CLIMATE: MULTI-FAITH

CONNECTIVITY (OVERALL)

STRONG **14%** — MEDIUM **35%** — WEAK **51%**

WARMTH TOWARD RELIGION

"Religion is good for people" — "Religion is harmful to people"

| 25% | 37% | 33% | 3% | 1% |

"Religion is important to society" — "Religion is a detriment to society"

| 23% | 36% | 35% | 5% | 1% |

Globally Connected

 55% "I feel connected to people around the world"

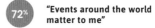 72% "Events around the world matter to me"

Relationally Connected

 31% "I often feel deeply cared for by those around me"

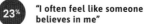 23% "I often feel like someone believes in me"

RELATIONSHIP TO RELIGION

"The Church is good for people" — "The Church is harmful to people"

| 20% | 30% | 44% | 5% | 1% |

"The Church is important to society" — "The Church is a detriment to society"

| 15% | 29% | 49% | 5% | 2% |

Attendance of Religious Respondents

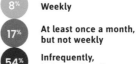
- 8% Weekly
- 17% At least once a month, but not weekly
- 54% Infrequently, but occasionally
- 22% Never

Do you feel like the Christian Church is making a difference on issues such as poverty and justice?

- 7% Definitely
- 51% Probably
- 34% Probably not
- 8% Definitely not

"My religious faith is very important in my life today"

 70%

"Because of my beliefs, it is important that I

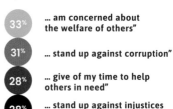
- 33% ... am concerned about the welfare of others"
- 31% ... stand up against corruption"
- 28% ... give of my time to help others in need"
- 28% ... stand up against injustices against individuals or groups"

OVERALL FAITH PROFILE:
UNITED KINGDOM

RELIGIOUS CLIMATE: SECULAR

CONNECTIVITY (OVERALL)

STRONG — **12%** — MEDIUM — **38%** — WEAK — **50%**

WARMTH TOWARD RELIGION

"Religion is good for people"   "Religion is harmful to people"

17%	23%	27%	20%	13%

"Religion is important to society"   "Religion is a detriment to society"

14%	23%	29%	21%	13%

Globally Connected

53% "I feel connected to people around the world"

80% "Events around the world matter to me"

Relationally Connected

24% "I often feel deeply cared for by those around me"

21% "I often feel like someone believes in me"

RELATIONSHIP TO RELIGION

"The Church is good for people"   "The Church is harmful to people"

19%	27%	30%	13%	11%

"The Church is important to society"   "The Church is a detriment to society"

16%	26%	32%	16%	10%

Attendance of Religious Respondents

15% Weekly

19% At least once a month, but not weekly

37% Infrequently, but occasionally

29% Never

Do you feel like the Christian Church is making a difference on issues such as poverty and justice?

11% Definitely
44% Probably
32% Probably not
14% Definitely not

"My religious faith is very important in my life today"

42%

"Because of my beliefs, it is important that I

41% ... am concerned about the welfare of others"

38% ... give of my time to help others in need"

37% ... stand up against injustices against individuals or groups"

OVERALL FAITH PROFILE:
UNITED STATES

RELIGIOUS CLIMATE:
CHRISTIAN

CONNECTIVITY (OVERALL)

STRONG **23%** — MEDIUM **38%** — WEAK **38%**

WARMTH TOWARD RELIGION

"Religion is good for people"　　　　　　　　"Religion is harmful to people"

| 29% | 28% | 22% | 14% | 7% |

"Religion is important to society"　　　　　　　　"Religion is a detriment to society"

| 26% | 26% | 25% | 14% | 9% |

Globally Connected

47% "I feel connected to people around the world"

81% "Events around the world matter to me"

Relationally Connected

36% "I often feel deeply cared for by those around me"

35% "I often feel like someone believes in me"

RELATIONSHIP TO RELIGION

"The Church is good for people"　　　　　　　　"The Church is harmful to people"

| 29% | 27% | 24% | 13% | 8% |

"The Church is important to society"　　　　　　　　"The Church is a detriment to society"

| 26% | 25% | 26% | 13% | 9% |

Attendance of Religious Respondents

26% Weekly

20% At least once a month, but not weekly

31% Infrequently, but occasionally

24% Never

Do you feel like the Christian Church is making a difference on issues such as poverty and justice?

16% Definitely
44% Probably
28% Probably not
13% Definitely not

"My religious faith is very important in my life today"

58%

"Because of my beliefs, it is important that I

52% ... am concerned about the welfare of others"

48% ... give of my time to help others in need"

46% ... stand up against injustices against individuals or groups"

Connect to Your Context Through Country Reports

The country profiles in this appendix are intended to give you a general overview of the connectivity levels and religious disposition among the 25 countries included in this study, building upon the themes explored at a global level. If you're looking for more details about the demographics and spiritual climate of your own region, *The Connected Generation* project also includes a series of country reports. Through country-specific data and analysis, expert commentary and contextualized field guides, you'll gain greater insight to help you begin to apply the research in your local ministry and community.

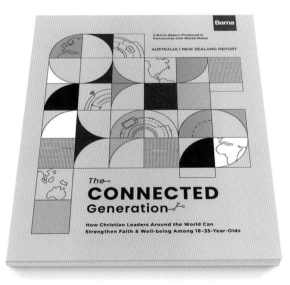

Learn more about these and other resources available through *The Connected Generation* project at **TheConnectedGeneration.com**.

Notes

1. Delaney Hall, "The Age of the Algorithm," 99% Invisible Podcast, Episode 274, September 5, 2017, https://99percentinvisible.org/episode/the-age-of-the-algorithm/.

2. Mark and I chatted about these five trends in an in-person interview, but he touches on many of the same themes in *Reappearing Church: The Hope for Renewal in the Rise of Our Post-Christian Culture* (Chicago: Moody Publishers, 2019).

3. David Kinnaman and Mark Matlock, *Faith for Exiles: 5 Ways for a New Generation to Follow Jesus in Digital Babylon* (Grand Rapids, MI: Baker, 2019), 16.

4. Looking at Pew Research Center's Global Attitudes Study, we can see that the 25 countries Barna sampled have generally high rates of internet connection and smart phone use. India and Indonesia fall to the bottom where only 25% and 30% (respectively) of adults either use the internet occasionally or have a smartphone. The United States, Canada, United Kingdom, Spain, Australia, Germany and South Korea all have the highest rates, each over 87% of the adult population; Jacob Poushter, Caldwell Bishop and Hanyu Chwe, "Social Media Use Continues to Rise in Developing Countries but Plateaus Across Developed Ones," Pew Research Center, June 19, 2018, https://www.pewresearch.org/global/2018/06/19/social-media-use-continues-to-rise-in-developing-countries-but-plateaus-across-developed-ones/; David Lazer, "The Rise of the Social Algorithm," Science Magazine, vol. 348 iss. 6239 (June 5, 2015) http://citeseerx.ist.psu.edu/viewdoc/download?doi=10.1.1.934.6292&rep=rep1&type=pdf; Aaron Smith, "Public Attitudes Toward Computer Algorithms," Pew Research Center, November 16, 2018, https://www.pewinternet.org/2018/11/16/public-attitudes-toward-computer-algorithms/; A.J. Agrawal, "What Do Social Media Algorithms Mean for You?" Forbes, April 20, 2016, https://www.forbes.com/sites/ajagrawal/2016/04/20/what-do-social-media-algorithms-mean-for-you/#2bce6796a515.

5. Jonathan Vespa, "Most Popular Living Arrangement Is Living with Parents," U.S. Census Bureau (blog), August 9, 2017, https://www.census.gov/library/stories/2017/08/young-adult-video.html; May Bulman, "Marriages Between Men and Women Hit Lowest Rate on Record," *The Independent*, February 28, 2018, https://www.independent.co.uk/news/uk/home-news/marriages-men-women-lowest-record-heterosexual-lgbt-ons-a8232751.html; Wendy Tuohy, "As Marriage Wanes and House Prices Rise, Young People Stay at Home," *The Sydney Morning Herald*, May 14, 2019, https://www.smh.com.au/lifestyle/life-and-relationships/as-marriage-wanes-and-house-prices-rise-young-people-stay-at-home-20190513-p51mtt.html.

6. Barna Group, *Gen Z: The Culture, Beliefs and Motivations Shaping the Next Generation*, (Ventura, CA: Barna, 2018).

7. PayPal, "PayPal Global Freelancer Survey," PayPal Stories (blog), March 1, 2018, https://www.paypal. com/stories/sea/paypal-global-freelancer-survey.

8. Jennifer Moss, "Helping Remote Workers Avoid Loneliness and Burnout," *Harvard Business Review*, November 30, 2018, https://hbr.org/2018/11/helping-remote-workers-avoid-loneliness-and-burnout.

9. Jason Compton, "How the World's Top 5 Nations in Education Handle Student Loan Debt," SoFi (blog), February 17, 2017, https://www.sofi.com/blog/how-top-countries-university-education-handle-student-loan-debt-repayment/; Joseph Chamie, "Student Debt Rising Worldwide," YaleGlobal Online, May 18, 2017, https://yaleglobal.yale.edu/content/student-debt-rising-worldwide.

10. Barna Group, *Christians at Work*, (Ventura, CA: Barna, 2018).

11. Barna Group, *Households of Faith*, (Ventura, CA: Barna, 2019).

12. Cheryl Doss et al., "The Role of Women in Agriculture," The Food and Agriculture Organization of the United Nations, Agricultural Development Economics Division, March 2011, http://www.fao.org/3/am307e/am307e00.pdf.

13. Luca Ventura, "The World's Richest and Poorest Countries 2019," *Global Finance*, April 22, 2019, https://www.gfmag.com/global-data/economic-data/worlds-richest-and-poorest-countries.

14. Deloitte. *The Deloitte Global Millennial Survey 2019*, 2019, https://www2.deloitte.com/global/en/pages/about-deloitte/articles/millennialsurvey.html.

15. Kashmira Gander, "Millennials Are the Most Anxious Generation, New Research Shows," *Newsweek*, May 9, 2018, https://www.newsweek.com/millennials-most-anxious-generation-new-research-shows-917095.

16. Young Women's Trust, "Young Women's Trust report reveals a generation losing hope, as millions of young people struggle to make ends meet," September 29, 2017, https://www.youngwomenstrust.org/what_we_do/media_centre/press_releases/673_ywt_report_reveals_a_generation_losing_hope.

17. Anne Helen Petersen, "How Millennials Became the Burnout Generation,"*Buzzfeed News*, January 5, 2019, https://www.buzzfeednews.com/article/annehelenpetersen/millennials-burnout-generation-debt-work.

18. Jean M. Twenge, "Have Smartphones Destroyed a Generation?" *The Atlantic*, September 2017, https://www.theatlantic.com/magazine/archive/2017/09/has-the-smartphone-destroyed-a-generation/534198/.

19. Laura Greenstein, "The Mental Health Benefits of Religion & Spirituality," National Association on Mental Illness (blog), December 21, 2016, https://www.nami.org/Blogs/NAMI-Blog/December-2016/The-Mental-Health-Benefits-of-Religion-Spiritual.

20. U.S. Central Intelligence Agency, "Africa: Kenya, the World Factbook," updated September 16, 2019, https://www.cia.gov/library/publications/the-world-factbook/geos/ke.html.

21. Bregtje Van der Haak and Richard Vijgen, "Atlas of Pentecostalism," Pulitzer Center, December 27, 2013, https://pulitzercenter.org/projects/africa-nigeria-pentecostal-christians-holy-spirit-global-religion-iconography-cartography-data-visualization.

22. Francis X. Rocca, Yelin Hong and Josh Ulick, "How the Catholic World Is Changing," *The Wall Street Journal*, n.d., http://graphics.wsj.com/catholics-world/.

23. John Burger, "The Catholic Population in Europe Has Plummeted, Pew Finds,"*Aleitia*, January 14, 2019, https://aleteia.org/2019/01/14/the-catholic-population-in-europe-has-plummeted-pew-finds/; Lydia Saad, "Catholics' Church Attendance Continues Downward Slide," *Gallup*, April 9, 2018, https://news.gallup.com/poll/232226/church-attendance-among-catholics-resumes-downward-slide.aspx.

24. Eve Fairbanks, "Behold, the Millennial Nuns," *Huffpost*, July 11, 2019, https://www.huffpost.com/highline/article/millennial-nuns/.

25. David Kinnaman and Mark Matlock, *Faith for Exiles: 5 Ways for a New Generation to Follow Jesus in Digital Babylon* (Grand Rapids, MI: Baker, 2019) 26–27.

26. Deloitte, "Deloitte Research Reveals 'a Generation Disrupted': Growing up in a World of Accelerated Transformation Leaves Millennials and Gen Zs Feeling Unsettled About the Future," news release, May 20, 2019, https://www2.deloitte.com/global/en/pages/about-deloitte/press-releases/deloitte-millennial-survey-research-reveals-gen-z-unsettled.html.

27. Anna Bahney, "What Millennials Really Want at Work," CNN Money, December 29, 2017, https://money.cnn.com/2017/12/29/pf/millennials-work.

28. Faith Survey, "Christianity in the UK," Faith Survey, https://faithsurvey.co.uk/uk-christianity.html.

29. Barna Group, *The State of Pastors* (Ventura, CA: Barna Group, 2017).

30. I've been influenced by Mark Sayers and Edwin Friedman when it comes to these characteristics.

Acknowledgments

Barna Group is incredibly grateful to World Vision, not only for their partnership on this massive study, but their global leadership in working with the poor and oppressed to promote human transformation, seek justice and bear witness to the good news of the kingdom of God. Our gratitude extends to the many World Vision staff members from more than 20 countries who supported this initiative through early input on the study formation, coordination of thought leaders and local contextualization. That lengthy list includes: Jenny Acosta, Asteria Aritonang, Marcela Ballestero, Christopher Baskeran, Allen Benjamin, Tennille Bergin, Amanda Bowman, David Brown, Nieves Carabaña, James Carroll, Chun-Sen Chang, Wesley Chen, Michael Chitwood, Eu-Lee Chng, Lilian Chung, João Diniz, Lauren Fisher, Anne Fleck, Jonathan Fletcher, Holly Frew, Marcus Frost, Javier Ruiz Gaitán, Jessica Galles, Ivan Gomez, Jun Goodness, Jason Graves, Sam Grimshaw, Cheryl Hotchkiss, KA Jayakumar, Caitie Johnston, Andrea Kaufmann, Kevin King, Esther Lehmann-Sow, André Mebold, Tim Middlemiss, Andrew Morley, Oliver Müller, David Muñoz, John Mwangi, John Northuis, James Pedrick, Tim Pilkington, Raymond Pu, Jill Roche, Raissa Rossiter, Edgar Sandoval Sr, Chris Schroeder, Harold Segura, Weijie Soh, Andrew Streat, Sony Thomas, Ruth Tormey, Michael Wenham, Clarice Ziller and more.

Our findings about the connected generation have been significantly strengthened by the feedback and grounded recommendations of ministers, activists, scholars and other experts spanning the globe, some of whom are featured within the pages of this report. A heartfelt thank you to those many commentators and contributors, including: Ruth Yimika Afolabi, Juliette Arulrajah, Jefferson Bethke, Abel Cheah, Jayakumar Christian, Daniel Flynn, Marco Tulio Gómez, Nicky Gumbel, Alan Jamieson, Krish Kandiah, James Mallon, Chine McDonald, Percy Mongwai, Daniel Muvengi, Lydia Mwaniki, David Oginde, Marco Oropeza, Stephen Proctor, Sifiso Pule, Natasha Sistrunk Robinson, Jackson Ole Sapit, Mark Sayers, Joy Beth Smith, Taya Smith, Wesley Teixeira, John Thornton Jr., Tracy Trinita, Tish Harrison Warren, Peter Wojcik and more. Additional thanks to McDonald and Kandiah for their early support and encouragement of this global project.

The Barna research team conducted this study with coordination by Brooke Hempell. Traci Hochmuth and Daniel Copeland led development of the questionnaire, with assistance from Susan Mettes. Copeland also served as lead analyst, with preliminary analysis contributed by Savannah Kimberlin, and provided data verification throughout. Alyce Youngblood managed editorial production and was lead writer on the manuscript, with additional data reporting from Joan Chen-Main, Ryan Hamm and Benjamin Howard. Roxanne Stone offered narrative direction and conducted interviews. David Kinnaman, with Aly Hawkins, wrote foundational pieces of the report. Marian Liautaud and Verónica Thames provided editorial and marketing support. Douglas Brown proofread the manuscript. OX Creative designed the cover. With initial visual direction from Chaz Russo, Lauren Harvill designed interior layout, and Annette Allen designed data visualizations. Brenda Usery managed production. Mallory Holt coordinated as project manager and assisted in organizing contributors. Joe Jensen managed the digital presence and webcast event for this project. Special thanks to Rick Ifland for his vision in extending Barna's reach internationally and Gareth Russell for spearheading the Barna Global effort. The project team wishes to thank our Barna colleagues—Amy Brands, Aidan Dunn, Janet Eason, Pam Jacob, Steve McBeth, Rhesa Storms, Jess Villa and Todd White—for their support as we've completed our largest study to date.

About the Project Partners

Barna Group is a research firm dedicated to providing actionable insights on faith and culture, with a particular focus on the Christian Church. Since 1984, Barna has conducted more than one million interviews in the course of hundreds of studies and has become a go-to source for organizations that want to better understand a complex and changing world from a faith perspective. Barna's clients and partners include a broad range of academic institutions, churches, nonprofits and businesses, such as Alpha, the Templeton Foundation, Fuller Seminary, the Bill and Melinda Gates Foundation, Maclellan Foundation, DreamWorks Animation, Focus Features, Habitat for Humanity, The Navigators, NBC-Universal, the ONE Campaign, Paramount Pictures, the Salvation Army, Walden Media, Sony and World Vision. The firm's studies are frequently quoted by major media outlets such as *The Economist*, BBC, CNN, *USA Today*, the *Wall Street Journal*, Fox News, *Huffington Post*, *The New York Times* and the *Los Angeles Times*.

www.barna.com

World Vision is a Christian relief, development and advocacy organization dedicated to working with children, families and communities to overcome poverty and injustice. As an international partnership of Christians, World Vision's mission is to work with the poor and oppressed to promote human transformation, seek justice and bear witness to the good news of the Kingdom of God. World Vision works with the most vulnerable children in the world so they can experience God's promise: life in all its fullness. Through the organization's work, every 60 seconds, a family gets water, a hungry child is fed, and a family receives the tools to overcome poverty. For nearly 70 years, World Vision has ministered alongside the Church to answer Jesus' call in Matthew 25—to care for the least of these. Together, with churches, their leaders and others, World Vision has impacted the lives of over 200 million vulnerable children by tackling the root causes of poverty.

www.wvi.org/connectedgeneration

Discover What's Working and Find Hope

Faith for Exiles *explores:*

- The biblical concept of exile as an essential framework for following Christ today
- Five research-based practices that cultivate faithfulness in digital Babylon
- How to prepare young Christians to be on mission with Jesus in the world
- How Jesus followers of all ages can thrive in our current exile

Faith For Exiles

5 Ways for a New Generation to Follow Jesus in Digital Babylon

David Kinnaman & Mark Matlock

The lighted rectangles in our pockets—smartphones and their bigger siblings, tablets and computers—have redefined so much about our lives, including spirituality and the pursuit of God. The ubiquity and power of the interconnected, digital age is affecting how we shape our souls. In other words, screens disciple. In a world where always-connected smart devices and search algorithms educate and entertain, digital Babylon is the new context for discipleship. That means we are all exiles now.

This practical and thought-provoking book reveals findings from a groundbreaking three-year research study. Barna president David Kinnaman teams up with Mark Matlock, founder of WisdomWorks, to enter the world of resilient young Christians and examine how they are sustaining faith.

Purchase at barna.com/ faithforexiles

Stay Informed About Global Trends

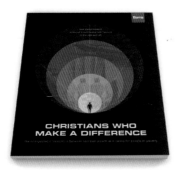

Christians Who Make a Difference
An examination of the unexpected connections between spiritual growth and caring for people in poverty.

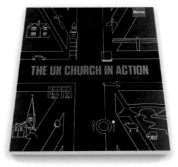

The UK Church in Action
Get to the heart of what mission means to Christians today as they fulfill their calling to be God's agents of change in the world.

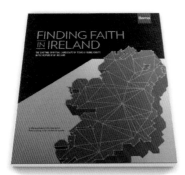

Finding Faith in Ireland
Go inside the minds of Irish youth as they wrestle with popular culture, societal expectations for success and the nation's transforming spiritual identity.

Transforming Scotland
A fascinating study that provides actionable insights into how to do ministry and be the Church in a rapidly secularizing context.

Knowledge to Lead with Confidence

Reviving Evangelism
A number of factors are curbing many Christians' enthusiasm for faith-sharing, including some non-Christians' suspicion of people of faith. Where does that leave evangelism?

Leadership Transitions
Change doesn't have to be a crisis. Research, insightful analysis and relatable case studies that help keep your church healthy through leadership change of all types.

Households of Faith
Discover the ways practicing Christians' core relationships engage them in a thoughtful, transformative faith—the kind that holds up to and is passed down over time.

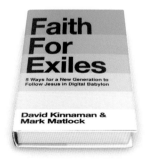

Faith for Exiles
Enter the world of resilient young adult Christians: learn how they are sustaining faith and find hope in all that God is doing among young disciples today.

AVAILABLE AT BARNA.COM/RESOURCES

What Can Barna Do For You?

When you need to make a decision, you want good information to guide you. You want a trusted advisor who knows the times. For more than 30 years, Barna has been providing reliable data and actionable insights to the leaders of some of the most influential organizations of our day. Whatever decision you're trying to make, Barna can help.

Custom Research

Accurate, timely and affordable research for organizations, faith leaders, entrepreneurs and innovators

Barna Polls

Shared-cost research that provides strategic insights about pastors or U.S. adults at minimal cost

Consulting

Actionable recommendations for your organization, grounded in research and an understanding of your context

Resources

Published research and insights for leaders and decision makers

Learn more about Barna's work at
barna.com
@barnagroup

Discover
Listening to understand your unique needs and expectations

Design
Determining the best questions and methodology to ensure meaningful and reliable findings

Gather
Ensuring that the data is accurate and representative of your key audiences

Analyze
Interpreting results and identifying key patterns, trends and insights

Deliver
Creating custom monographs, reports or presentations to fit your needs

Advise
Applying Barna's decades of knowledge and experience to give you confidence to take action